From The Brink Of Death

By

Tabitha Marie Ann McGee

Copyright

Copyright © 2025 Tabitha Marie Ann McGee

Published by

All rights reserved. No part of this book may be reproduced or transmitted in any form or by any means, electronic or mechanical, including photocopying, recording, or by any information storage and retrieval system, without written permission from the publisher and author

Dedication

To the two people in my life that have proven time and time again that they believe in me. One of you taught me how to be strong and keep going, even before we truly knew each other. Another, convinced me to write this story.

Table of Contents

Prologue 6
Chapter 1 7
Chapter 2 10
Chapter 3 12
Chapter 4 14
Chapter 5 16
Chapter 6 19
Chapter 7 21
Chapter 8 24
Chapter 9 26
Chapter 10 29
Chapter 11 33
Chapter 12 36
Chapter 13 38
Chapter 14 41
Chapter 15 43
Chapter 16 46
Chapter 17 50
Chapter 18 55
Chapter 19 59
Chapter 20 64
Chapter 21 67
Chapter 22 73
Chapter 23 77
Chapter 24 83

Chapter 25 93
Chapter 26 104
Chapter 27 107
Chapter 28 112
Chapter 29 120
Chapter 30 124

Prologue

I'm the villain, or at least, that's the picture people often paint, and my story is not for the faint of heart.

I was born in a small town, in the middle of summer, on a Monday that I don't remember, to a woman I know nothing about, and in due time, the name she had given me would also be taken away.

She had been gifted, like me, and before I was born, she faced a rather tough decision: let me live or send me to our ancestors. So, my mother did what any intuitively guided woman would have done in the late '90s and went to find a tarot reader. Although I'll never know what she was told, it led to this moment in time.

For protective reasons, the names of the people who were once in my life have been changed, and no locations are disclosed. What I am about to tell you is quite difficult; some memories have been lost to time, and others still haunt me

Be prepared.

Chapter 1

As I've already said, remembering my mother's face is obsolete. I've tried many times, though it doesn't matter much anymore. All I know is that she was attuned to several complex and unique spiritual gifts, which I inherited at birth, leading to a rather unique life experience.

However, my earliest memories of her are of when she walked away, and back then, my tiny three-year-old mind couldn't comprehend what was happening; all I could do was wiggle in the arms of a dark-cloaked stranger and scream at her retreating back, "Mommy, why are you leaving?"

As I grew older, I inevitably added the mental note, If you had ever loved us, you would've stayed, but in my mind, she had abandoned me and my brother, who had only been about one year old at the time.

We were put into the system, and from there, the nightmares began. Although there were some good moments, they were so few and far between that they've nearly been forgotten.

By the time my brother, Noah, was three and I was five, a seemingly nice, sweet elderly couple had taken us in as foster children. They also had another foster child, Daniel, who was just a tad older than me. Some days there was peace and pleasantries; those would pass before my young, bright eyes in a blur of vibrant colors. Other days were rather gloomy and hard to forget; much like the times I always seemed to get in trouble for things I didn't even do.

As toddlers, Noah and I were unsurprisingly over-mature for our ages, and we eventually convinced our foster parents, Joan and Mark, to let us each have a pet. They were bunnies, kept in covered cages outdoors, but they were ours. My pet had a beautiful chocolate-brown coat, and I instantly chose to name her Princess.

My brother's pet was white with brown spots, and he simply chose the name Power Ranger. I thought it was strange, but since he was obsessed with the show, it made perfect sense.

Eventually, my brother lost interest and blatantly discarded his pet rabbit, and no matter how persistent I was, Noah didn't care. That led to the morning I found that Power Ranger had passed away.

That morning was cold, and the sun had not yet risen, but it wasn't yet cold enough for the first frost of winter. Still, my little hands were tightly wrapped in woolen mittens, and a thick coat bunched around my shoulders. I was terrified of the dark, so I kept as close to the house as I could, silently praying just as my only friend had instructed me.

Every time I spoke about my friend, they thought I was making things up. I remember being asked to describe him once, and as I've aged, I've noticed he's gradually chosen to do the same. Although as an infant child, I never saw his wings.

My friend watched as I continued moving forward, and as night slowly drifted into dawn, my tiny hands finally grasped the cover enclosed both cages. The smell hit me instantly, a pungent mix of spoiled meat and decay. I quickly covered my mouth before standing on my tiptoes to see inside. Instinct made my eyes dart around until they landed on the beautiful chocolate-brown fur of my bunny, peering back at me. Her eyes held something I would only later recognize as contempt. In the cage next to her lay a mass of unmoving white with brown spots, covered in maggots and worms, his glossed-over eyes still wide open, the look of distress forever etched in my mind. I screamed and darted back toward the house. Power Ranger was buried that same day.

Shortly afterward, Princess mysteriously learned how to open the feeder attached to her cage and escaped during the first frost. When she was finally found, I was devastated, but no amount of my insistence that the cage had been locked was heard.

As punishment for lying, I was dragged into the downstairs living room, made to stand barefoot on the wooden table, and my legs were pulled from underneath me. The back of my tender five-year-old head and rear end hit the floor hard, but with each scream or cry, the length of time would only increase. So, I learned rather quickly to suffer in absolute silence.

Chapter 2

Fast forward a few more years, and by now I am seven and Noah is five. I've gotten good at coming up with excuses for the bruises, as well as for my refusal to eat or be relatively social with my peers.

However, I made sure that Noah hardly ever had a scratch on him; it's always been my job as the oldest to look after my kid brother, even if he can sometimes be mistaken for foolish. Plus, I'd gotten used to receiving punishments, which by now were on a rotating cycle, mostly consisting of three main things: running barefoot through pine needles, having my legs pulled from underneath me, or simply going hungry. It was bearable knowing he wasn't going through the same.

Then, somehow, against my original insistence, the pretty blond girl who lived near us started considering herself my friend. We were close in age and practically inseparable, especially when there wasn't school to attend, often playing childish pranks on each other.

I can still remember fondly one such occasion in the spring, when I had her very convinced that there was a monster in the pond who would have dragged her under if she dared get near it.

That monster turned out to be a snapping turtle as big as the inside of a small wheelbarrow; we had lovingly named him Mr. Snappy before he grew too big and scared us so much that we had no choice but to eat him. I've never wanted a turtle after that.

Back then, there were four of us: I, the blond-haired girl from next door who I discovered was named Lily, my brother Noah, and Daniel, who was probably the worst influence on the plane. We were all in the system together, but I'll never forget the joy we each shared upon finding out we would be adopted on or around the exact same day.

Chapter 3

In August of 2006, Noah and I were officially moved into what was lovingly nicknamed our forever house. It was two stories tall with a wrap-around porch, a long steep driveway that had once been blacktop, and hope, because it was the most beautiful place I had ever seen. In my little mind, I thought it was a palace: my pretty bright yellow and fading white palace. This was also the day I had my first encounter with a dog and came to realize rather quickly that I prefer cats.

Upon entering the house, being freaked out by the friendly unfamiliar pups, and earning myself a nickname that would follow me into my later years, our first official project began: we got to pick our very own rooms.

I had originally chosen the former master bedroom downstairs, mostly because I'd never been in a room that big. It had both a walk-in closet and a huge bathroom. Noah's original choice was the tinier room at the top of the stairs, directly above the formal living and dining room area. It had a bird's-eye view of the road leading toward and away from the house, and was directly across the hall from our parents' room.

Our parents. I remember daydreaming about how beautiful my new home was and that my new dad seemed nice.

Sometimes, I can catch myself still wishing those rose-colored glasses hadn't snapped off so easily. For eight-year-old me, it was a new form of deviation once they did. However, it wouldn't be long until I was asking the age-old question,

"When can I see my real mommy?"

And getting those adult-flavored lies only a traumatized child would detect. They liked to skirt around every excuse, under both the sun and moon, but nothing seemed to truly fit right, and eventually, I would learn to stop asking the living for the truth.

Although in the early days there wasn't anything bad; sometimes there were spontaneous family trips, and there was always something new to learn. Much like our first and only time on the top of Pikes Peak, where my new mom, Lyann, inevitably freaked out because my little brother, Noah, had a nosebleed from the thin oxygen.

Then there were our family trips to Florida, where my ears burned so badly they still have faint scars, and I somehow convinced my new dad, Paul, to not only pick up seashells with me along the beach for hours on end but also to have all ten of his toes painted bright pink; and he actually did it.

This was also the same summer when I first recognized how differently I looked compared to my new family. Anyone who noticed us would have seen quite an interesting sight: an older mixed native man happily going along with whatever a young, fair-skinned child asked.

Chapter 4

If you're wondering where it all went wrong, I'll tell you. It was at Thanksgiving dinner, during one of our first years as a family. It had only been a few weeks since I'd been instructed to change my name, and I was still trying to figure out why. I rather liked having two first names that was traditional.

Anyway, there were several people in our house, and that meant only one thing: we could go into the formal rooms without getting into trouble. There was also a delicious and amazing home-cooked Thanksgiving spread. Believe me, we pride ourselves on knowing our way around any kitchen. That's why I learned so early, and from the very best, my auntie Claire, my dad, and my Nona.

However, even though I was happy with my new family, my growing persistence to see, hear, and speak with my real mother was still very present; it didn't help that our origins Noah's and mine were the main topic of discussion. Everyone wanted to know exactly what, or even if, we remembered anything. Well, my new mom and I piped up at the exact same time; to my horror, Lyann started claiming some terribly hurtful and blatant untruths about the woman who had risked her life to give birth to me. Before I understood what I'd done, I reminded her that it was unbecoming to spread falsities.

This did not go over well, and I was quickly dragged into my bedroom by the ear. She got in my face and told me never to behave that way again; then the back of my head was forced into the wall, and all former perceptions about her completely shattered.

The incident was over in a matter of seconds, and I soon watched her snake a dazzling smile across her harsh German features. It was the exact same smile I would have easily fallen for a moment prior. Only now, I started to notice that it never reached her eyes. I was told to pretend that nothing had happened and was made to apologize for my actions.

From that night forward, it soon became apparent that she no longer liked me but wouldn't do anything past childlike bullying and manipulation. This kind of thing went on for years, and eventually, I simply fell into a new pattern.

Which consisted of being forced to take medication I never needed, which later led to an addiction I struggled with but broke free from; running excessively, this time with shoes on; frequent starvation, which seemed to be a fan favorite; and being shoved into things.

Pretty soon, I hit a downward spiral, mainly because I had absolutely nobody to confide in. Lily wasn't around anymore, and every attempt to make friends with my new peers didn't last long. It was almost like I wasn't allowed.

Chapter 5

The longest time I had a friend was between sixth and seventh grade. He was a very outspoken boy with curly red hair and black square-rimmed glasses. We would often sit by each other during recess and talk about what we wanted to be as adults.

Although, in the back of my heart, I managed to keep alive the one thing I was led to believe I'd never be good enough for, my common answer to this question would have been a chef or restaurant owner.

His dream? To be an Air Force pilot.

Except life played a cruel hand, and his was sadly cut short by a terminal illness, making an unforeseen U-turn to reclaim him back over to the other side leaving me alone once again.

The morning he passed away, I was sitting in first period French class, and we had just started watching a movie. Even though I had this dark feeling of foreboding looming over everything, I still tried my best to ignore it. That was until the phone started to ring, and I found myself tuning into what Madam was saying rather than the picture being projected onto the whiteboard. It was obvious from her tone that something was wrong, but I kept trying to make out what the other person was saying. I knew it had to be Father Marcus on the other end of the line; something simply told me that it was our school's pastor she was speaking with, but what were they saying?

Soon, Madam ended the call, and I tried my very best to pretend I had been paying attention to the movie. As she crept up behind me, I was told to gather my things and leave for the day.

Everything felt surreal when I exited the trailer and began heading toward the main office, where the guidance counselor's door was softly shut behind me.

You could have cut the tension in the room with a dull knife. So, I tried a joke, but it didn't work. After a few rounds of being told to sit and demanding an explanation, I heard the words that shook me to my little core:

"...We have no other way to tell you this..."

He didn't need to continue. I already knew that Joey was gone. I'd felt the familiar shift of death that morning but hadn't wanted to accept it until I was forced to face reality. I cried on the phone with my dad, and he gave me two choices: either I could return home and cry to my heart's content, or I could stay and attempt to finish out the day to the best of my ability. Since it had already started, I decided to stay.

At recess, I opted to go to the same spot Joey and I always had; it was now a lonely swing, and I sat there idly by myself. The tears had long dried by this point, but I still kept my head down close to my chest. Silently, I prayed to whoever was listening, and for some strange reason, I requested something I'm still unsure I was supposed to. Back then, my little brain had no perception of what

I'd just done, but it was already too late, someone had heard me and they answered.

It wouldn't be long until I felt a wave of calming heat wash over me and noticed everything fade into varying shades of grey. I heard no sounds from the other kids at play and paid no mind to the outside world. Almost instinctively, I looked up at the sky and came face to face with a person standing, shrouded in nearly blinding light.

Instead of seeing, I felt this man smile down at me as he said something without speaking a word; all I could manage was a meek nod, but this ended up being the response he needed. He smiled at me once again and disappeared. After this, everything seemed to return to the way it had been all the same, yet entirely different.

A few days passed, and plans were quickly made for me to transfer schools; in almost no time, I was in a brand-new place, right in the middle of the year. Collectively, everything else had also changed. We'd gone from the family farm into a small house in the suburbs of a city I didn't want to be in. I began to fold in on myself a lot more, mostly so nobody would feel the need to get close to me again.

Days were filled with the same mundane habits of going to school, struggling through the motions, and trying to detach from everything as much as possible. By this point, I was fourteen and solely dependent on not-so-clean habits to help numb me out; sometimes taking more than what was recommended and lying if I happened to get caught. This often turned me into a hollow shell, but at least I was able to move.

Chapter 6

In the blink of an eye, I had aged once again, and by now I was sixteen, almost seventeen; my life kept spiraling downhill. It was one of those days where I didn't want to deal with or feel anything, and that's when the first started.

I'm not sure exactly how, but I remember sitting at the dining room table with an open history book and a blank notepad. It was blatantly obvious that I was actively procrastinating, but I truly didn't see the point to any of this; then the she-devil walked in. Now, I know that perception isn't fair, but that's exactly how I saw her back then.

Our relationship was often jagged and non-existent at best. The mom I had once hoped for had turned out to be a childish fairytale, just like everything else.

She was already pissed about something, so seeing me procrastinating simply pushed her over the edge. The next thing I knew, we were screaming at each other, and then she was pushing me down the stairs.

I wore violet colored, slim-rimmed glasses back then, and she opted to take them off my head before proceeding to break them and throw them down the stairs after me. I had short, almost boyish-style hair, and a small wire frame, due to the fact I'd always had to steal food from the kitchen when she wasn't looking. Once again, I was told there'd be three more days without food, and that I'd be sleeping on the downstairs living room floor.

Of course, these things only seemed to happen when Dad would be at work or away on the farm. I guess, you can say, he sort of became my safe person. We'd often go everywhere together, and our conversations ranged from the craziest of conspiracy theories to pretty much whatever you could think of, within reason. There was hardly a dull moment when it was just me and my Dad.

That night, I struggled to fall asleep on the cold concrete, as she'd already taken everything, including the stereo Dad had given me. Back then, music was my only outlet, so in my only form of rebuttal, I'd hidden my old alarm clock in the only place she wouldn't think to look. It was pink and white, hardly picking up a signal, but that was enough for me. I plugged it in and turned the volume extremely low, as I'd be the only one able to hear it anyway.

After switching it on, a smile crept onto my face because it still worked. I turned through channels of static and noise until the familiar sound of a certain bass guitar came through. A wave of instant calm washed over me as the lead singer's gentle voice lulled through the old clock.

Chapter 7

A few moments later, I ended up meeting a very different companion, much like the one from when I was a child; although she was kind to me, she was shrouded in complete darkness.

Quietly, as if under a trance, I began tracing an outline made entirely from my own blood. I harmed myself frequently back then, and to say I had no idea what I was doing is a bit presumptuous. I'd been working with both Angels and Ascended for years, but what I felt that night wasn't from them.

As future scenes began to play out in my mind's eye, pure blackened rage enveloped me, that wasn't mine. Lying on the cold concrete, I finally began to understand the motive behind every action, and seeing as we both wanted something, a silent pact was quickly made. Seconds later, the implosion of what seemed to be a writhing ball of moltan fire took hold inside of me as she made herself at home. Once again, I felt everything shift.

The next few days passed by in a sharp haze as I was no longer allowed to numb myself out using any of my previous methods. However, a scene was still made when pretending to take them, followed by an immediate excuse to use the downstairs bathroom and discard everything using the toilet. As days continued to pass by in this new routine, soon another discussion between my folks occurred.

The topic? Me.

Paul wanted me to go back up to the farm, and finish schooling in my hometown. She didn't like the idea at first. Then he expressed to Lyann how he felt the city was making me depressed, and he wasn't too fond of the way that I was turning out. She still refused to care until coming to the realization this meant we no longer had to see each other every day.

Which was fine, I didn't want to be around either. The minute I graduated high school, I'd leave and none of them would ever see me again. If I had to, I'd cut contact, and for the most part, I have. All things considered, it hasn't been a loss on my end.

I'd nearly been successful at remaining isolated and keeping up the invisible kid routine. Which is exactly what it seemed like she wanted. This worked like a charm on most people. Although, there were a few exceptions, and somehow I'd managed to acquire fellowship from three or four other misfits. We had the same taste in rock and metal bands, and a few of us even bonded over our shared traumatic experiences. I didn't want to leave them behind, but it wasn't my choice to make.

One day quickly led to another, and soon it was the end of another hellish year of high school. We gathered at our lockers and pulled out stacks of crumpled papers, battered notebooks, and binders covered in painstakingly crafted sharpie graffiti that we'd drawn on throughout the semester; someone grabbed a large black trash bin and we dumped it all. It was the closest feeling to freedom I'd gotten in a while. Soon, we walked down the stairs and out of the building for the last time.

I was smiling and laughing, which is something I didn't really do. Then one of the misfits got a bright idea and passed it to another one, and before I could make sense of it, someone had already picked me up and proceeded to run off with me. His name was Thomas, and we'd had a few classes together that year. I was still laughing as I fell over when he failed to put me down on my feet. It was a bittersweet moment; I'd finally found people who cared and that I cared for, and I knew in my heart we would probably never see each other again. I hoped that he couldn't see my tears as Thomas pulled me into a warm hug, and as the lump in my throat began to tighten, we all exchanged hugs one last time.

There was Pierce, this beautiful, wild, and badass girl who was always getting dress coded for her unique choices in fashion. Then Alex, the long-haired gothic boy who wore a literal trench coat during winter, and knew me better than anyone. I'd secretly placed a bet that they would've started dating by this time last fall and sadly, I had lost.

After giving everyone hugs, we each went our separate ways, but still I didn't have the heart to tell them, by midday tomorrow I'd be back in the middle of nowhere. So, I left it alone.

Chapter 8

I quickly got packed with my book bag and small sack of clothes; I felt a wave of bittersweet joy to be headed back up. The city and these suburbs just weren't my thing. I wanted to be able to hop over a fence again.

Dad decided to go with me, and it was long before conversations began flowing like they used to. We played our road games and tried to guess how distracted other drivers might be, by simply watching their tires. On the way, we also decided to try and find one of those old-fashioned, seemingly timeless stops for food, and it took a couple of tries, but eventually we came across our old favorite.

A small place along an old back road; they had the best cheesy fries and old-fashioned root beer. We'd stopped here a few years prior, after I'd just gotten my wisdom teeth pulled. Back then, Dad had relentlessly teased me by eating my favorite cheesy fries and a barbecue pulled pork sandwich, directly in front of me. Except, what he didn't know wouldn't hurt him; the owner had hidden a tiny cherry at the bottom of my plain vanilla shake, and the pain had been worth it.

It didn't take us long to finish what we could, save the rest, and get back on the road. Soon we reached the turn onto the familiar grey gravel, and Dad rolled both windows down. I stuck my right hand out of the passenger side and let the wind whip through my fingers. Hardly anyone used this route, and that's why it was our favorite.

The scenery from the fields was always gorgeous, and it never mattered if the crop was ready to be harvested or if it'd been recently sowed. I never got tired of looking.

A smile flashed across my face as I watched crop fields turn into green livestock pastures, and I knew we were getting close. Although, reluctantly, that meant I had to put my arm back in the truck as Dad rolled up the windows. We passed by the neighbors, where at one point I'd accidentally uprooted their entire mailbox when I was thirteen; it was one time, and I made them a brand-new one afterwards.

In my defense, the person teaching me how to drive didn't have a lick of sense and shouldn't have screamed as I was trying to back up.

My stomach did a twist, and I knew what Dad was doing; it was time to visit my Auntie and Uncle. In private, I still sometimes think he thought his sister was a bit strange, but it's most likely just a sibling trait. I thought my baby brother was an annoying and spoiled brat sometimes; I loved him nonetheless and always will.

Chapter 9

No sooner had Dad's black truck stopped in front of the back porch, than Auntie's head stuck out from the screen door. A smile that never quite found its way into her eyes etched itself across her aging native features as she quickly realized who it was. After slamming the truck door closed, I composed myself and started walking towards the wooden steps. We each walked up the front porch, Dad always letting me go first, and Auntie Claire opened the door with a hug ready for each of us. Upon entry, our shoes had to come off or we wouldn't be allowed to proceed further. These had always been the rules. So, I took off my old sneakers before stepping into my Auntie's embrace. She smelled like soul food, and I was silently grateful that she'd been one of my teachers in the kitchen.

Over her shoulders, I spotted my Uncle Thomas. He was sitting at a stool, on his phone, with a glass of homemade sweet iced tea in front of him. He looked up as I sat down and smiled; we exchanged pleasantries as Dad and Auntie Claire made their way into the kitchen.

There wasn't anything like the energy from that day. Once again, Auntie had made too much food for so few people, and as we sat around the kitchen table, I became the topic of discussion. Again.

Dad wanted me to live back on family land, and I was more than happy to oblige. It didn't take much convincing either. Auntie Claire started in on the age-old lie that they were missing me, and I simply played along.

Soon, my Dad stood up from the table and we exchanged a warm smile; it'd been pre-decided that I wouldn't be staying in my Auntie's home. I'd be staying in the forever home, by myself.

After all, I was nearly an adult now, and if there wasn't work or school, I'd spend my time on the farm anyway. It was my sanctuary and the only place I felt safe in the entire world.

I stood and walked with my Dad towards the door, then he took a half turn and said to me,

"Kiddo, prove them wrong."

Not much of a surprise, but there weren't too many people who thought I'd even graduate high school. Can't say that I blame them. Between the drug use, lack of motivation, and refusal to be considered even somewhat normal, I wasn't exactly put in a decent spotlight. I gave Dad a hug and buried my face in his chest.

Soon though, I watched his truck practically flying down the gravel and knew it was time to head over to the house. I gave my Auntie Claire another hug and waved goodbye to my Uncle Thomas, as he didn't like to be touched; then there was the choice of two different routes to take.

My Aunt had told me to go along the road, but I really missed cutting through the pasture; halfway down the driveway, I turned back to make sure nobody was watching, then cut across the yard towards the chicken coop. This was the route I'd always taken as a child and whenever I felt like sneaking over to snatch some of Auntie's crop. It's not like she missed it, and she'd always blame an imaginary rodent for getting past her dummy baits.

I hadn't truly smiled in years, and it spread widely across my face after moving past the chickens and out of the treeline.

On the other side of a gravel road, named after the man himself, sat my grandfather's house. He'd built it with his own two hands and it was here that he'd helped my grandma raise three children. I'd heard so many stories growing up that it almost felt like everything had happened to me.

Chapter 10

My Dad is the youngest of three, with my Auntie Claire being the middle child, and my crazy Uncle Oscar, who'd quickly become my second-best friend, as the oldest.

Oftentimes, when Dad and I would take the drive out to visit Uncle Oscar, I'd run up and steal the hat from off his bald, shiny head. He never minded, and it would come as no surprise that I was mostly raised by my Dad, grandfather, grandmother, and Uncle Oscar. We'd practically go everywhere together, and no day would be complete without some southern redneck fun.

I put my bags over my shoulder and stepped out into the middle of the road. Hell, there was never traffic out here, so it didn't matter.

As I made my way to see Grandpa, a fresh wave of contentment washed over me that I hadn't felt in years. I looked out at the old pond and couldn't help but wonder how to stop time. For lack of a better term, everything was simply perfect. Pretty soon, I found myself walking down the gravel drive toward his home and felt a twinge of longing.

He'd helped to raise three kids in this house, and Grandma Rose was no longer on the farm.

Of course, they'd originally had to live in the workshop, as it'd been the only building Grandpa finished, but then sometime during the late '70s or early '80s, he'd finally gotten the house done. Every time I looked, it felt like going back in time.

Sadly, Grandma had been placed into a nursing home when I was twelve, and she didn't come out. Her mind was completely gone, and despite his insistence, everyone knew that Grandpa just couldn't keep up with her anymore. She'd had this habit of simply walking off, and right before we came to accept that there was no longer a choice, Dad found her walking up the driveway. She was carrying two pairs of heels in a plastic sack and dressed like a woman from the 1980s who was going to her job at the factory. She'd even claimed to be heading into town, and that was a sad day; for it marked the beginning of a rapid family dynamic decline.

As quickly and quietly as possible, I snuck down the concrete steps to the back door. Nobody ever used the front; it was simply for decoration or special occasions. Just as I'd suspected, Grandpa was watching the news, completely muted. He had hearing aids but always made an excuse not to wear them. Grandma Rose used to say that he didn't have hard hearing, it was just very selective.

I knocked a few times, and he finally turned around. His baby-blue eyes lit up when he saw me, and a smile flashed across his aged native features.

He got up from his chair to let me in, and at this point, I'd been smiling so much that my cheeks were beginning to hurt. After the door was unlocked, Grandpa immediately opened his arms for a hug, and I happily obliged. Hardly anything had changed, and for a moment I could've almost convinced myself that Grandma Rose was either cleaning upstairs or hiding somewhere.

After giving Grandpa a hug, I sat down in the folding chair across from him, and we began to catch up on everything. I remember looking at him and feeling peace.

His eyes were the exact same shape and color as Dad's: two nearly crystal-like pale blue orbs. It's always been my favorite feature, as eyes are the windows to one's very soul.

Sadly, darkness began to spread, and soon it was time to head back home. I stood and walked the few steps to give Grandpa another hug; his face became serious as he warned me not to cut through the fields this late. All I could do was agree, and pretty soon I was walking up to the house and punching in the code for the side door. I was greeted by vast empty space and sighed, completely content. Being alone has a calming effect on me, and what nearly seventeen-year-old kid doesn't want an entire house to themselves?

Upon entry, I quickly punched in the code to stop the alarm before it started and locked the door behind me. Then I hurried up the small flight of stairs and towards the kitchen. Unfortunately, nothing interested me, so I headed up the second flight of stairs and into my room. At first, it'd been my brother's, but he'd begged and pleaded until I finally agreed to switch with him.

His loss.

I've always loved the sunrise in the morning. Seeing another beautiful painting that's been created by Source Divine is the best start to any day, and even if it turns into a bad one, there's always something to look forward to tomorrow.

Chapter 11

It almost seemed like the very next day, but soon enough, it was time to go to yet another school. This one was smaller than the others I'd been to, and the energy felt different. It wasn't hollow ground, but it felt very close. Auntie Claire went with me on the first day, and to say that was embarrassing is the understatement of the century. Despite her fuss, I still wanted to hide in my favorite band's hoodie, and, as suspected, yours truly was the only outcast. Everywhere I looked, there was a mix of boots, blue jeans, and flannel. I felt like an outsider in my ripped black skinnies and vans. So, I kept my head down and turned up the volume in my earbuds.

We headed toward the main office, where the woman behind the counter reluctantly gave me the sheet for my classes. At least this time, I hadn't moved in the middle of the year. That first day was brutal, though.

It took a solid ten minutes to figure out that my locker was upstairs, and then another five to learn that my first class was right beside my freaking locker. Just my luck, right? It was also English, and to make things worse, I was late.

Everyone stared when I walked in, and you could clearly hear the metal band blasting in my earbuds. I nodded a quick hello toward my teacher and made my way to the back of the class. Nobody bothered to say anything, but they sure loved to stare.

It felt like I was in some sort of freaky spotlight, and it wasn't until the teacher cleared her throat that they stopped scrutinizing me with their strange, bright, life-filled eyes. It seemed like everyone I caught a glimpse of still had that fire in their heart, it hadn't been forcibly extinguished; lucky bastards.

I kept my head down and pulled out one of my earbuds so I could hear everything; hindsight not being so twenty-twenty, it probably would've been better just to keep it in because these kids were anything but nice. Then, against my growing desire to escape, my teacher did the worst thing imaginable and called me up to introduce myself. From first impressions, I thought she was dressed too elegantly to be an English teacher in a small, one-stop-sign town, but I still hoped we'd be able to get along. I stood and took a quick breath before sending up a quiet prayer that this would be enough.

"Hi, I'm… and I just moved back up here."

It wasn't. Immediately, before I could try to sit down again, she started to bombard me with questions, and I gave each of them a single-word response. After a good few minutes, she reluctantly gave in and let me sit down.

Right off the bat, I made a mental note of which teachers I'd get along with and which I wouldn't. Then, by 2:45 in the afternoon, I was more than ready to leave.

I absolutely hated my new school not the building, just the people. They were all pretending to be someone else, somebody perfect, and all I wanted to do was go back to my sanctuary so I could scream.

Then, a voice caught my attention, and I turned to see a strange yet familiar face, with long, pretty blond hair. She was rather short and had a bright, optimistic, rosy smile.

"You're new here, aren't you? Nice to meet you, I'm…"

Drowning out everything else, I focused on trying to figure out why her voice was so familiar, but I couldn't seem to place it. Then I realized she'd stopped talking and was staring at me. Shit. I smiled and looked down at my scuffed vans which seemed to have a mind of their own, steadily kicking at the unmovable linoleum tiles and hoping she'd simply walk away.

She didn't. Instead, she'd opted to walk beside me, and when I reached for my bag, she reached for hers. Great, we're locker partners, and I'd completely ignored her. I felt like the biggest jerk in existence, but when I turned to try and say something, she was already walking down the stairs.

Shrugging it off, I grabbed what I needed for homework, slammed my door shut, and followed suit. By the time I made it back to the farm, I was starting to feel like myself.

Chapter 12

Months passed by, and soon it was springtime again. I'd somehow convinced them to let me out so I could hurry up and leave. That meant only a few weeks left, and all I had to get through was prom and graduation.

It had been a whirlwind of emotions and typical drama that I'd initially wanted to avoid much like a particular group of boys who'd made it their mission during the semester to hassle me. Honestly, I just wanted to get out of there. Most days, I was either too stoned to deal with it or simply didn't care. We all have our vices, and mine had gone from prescriptions that did nothing but numb me out to a plant that made me hungry and giggly.

A few days before graduation, I was stoned and determined to have a somewhat decent day. Then I climbed up the stairs and came face to face with Josh, one of my biggest bullies. Great. He often teased me about anything and everything his microscopic brain could think of, but today he simply flashed a smile and knocked my Sharpie graffiti binders out of my hands. I took a deep breath and glared; we didn't exchange words, but I really wanted to hit him.

All but a few papers were scattered between linoleum tiles and at the top of the stairs. So, I waited until he walked away to retrieve them. Then, I made my way to my locker and shoved everything inside. After that, I went through the motions, and before long, the bell for the last period rang.

I smiled at my teacher, Mr. E., who'd actually been nice to me, and gathered up my books to leave. He'd decided that the final day wasn't a "teach day" and instead opted to play his guitar after teaching us how to play poker. So, it was still shaping up to be a somewhat decent day, despite what had happened that morning.

However, as I walked down the hall, something felt different, and before too long, I'd left my body unattended.

You're always warned before astral projecting for the first time: never leave your body unattended and always have the quickest route back. I'd grown up hearing Nona's warnings and stories. How could I have forgotten?

Well, I guess it didn't matter now. Soon I was standing outside a gorgeous golden library with ancient and intricately crafted doors. It wouldn't be until later that I'd discover it was called The Library of Souls.

Here, Akashic records are kept for anything and everyone; you can seek knowledge without hassle on whatever you wish. You can seek out the hidden truth. It was another sanctuary. Thankfully, it was only a quick trip, and I soon found myself back in my body, standing in front of an open locker. After shaking off the cold that often comes with returning, I shoved some books in my bag, slammed the door, and headed to choir, my last class. The best is always saved for last.

Chapter 13

Finally, graduation day had arrived, and this would mark the third time I'd worn a dress in my entire life. The first was my Holy Communion as a child, the second was a long baby pink dress for prom that I'd been bribed with food to wear, and this one was a mix of blue, white, and green borrowed from Lyann.

I'd decided to dress conservatively and, once again, was made to look like an outsider especially when I got a peek at what some of the other girls were wearing. A few had decided to go with pajamas, and others had hardly anything on.

After walking into the school building, we all gathered in the cafeteria for food before the ceremony began. I didn't make small talk with my peers, and none of them bothered to do the same. They kept to their circle of friends, and I remained in happy solitude.

Soon, the bell rang, and we all went up to our arranged places. The girls headed into the choir rooms to don our caps and gowns, while the boys went into carpentry. They wore these dark blue cloaks with the school's logo printed in white on the front. Then, we filed out and created a single line, heading straight for the gymnasium.

Once we all sat down in the reserved front middle rows, the ceremony began. I drowned out most of it until my favorite teacher took the podium to give his speech. He told everyone how proud he was to have known them and reminded us not to be strangers after we left.

He tried to give us his best advice, and for some reason, it felt like he was talking to me and no one else. If I could remember what he said, that would truly be a blessing, but sadly, I can't recall.

Eventually, it was diploma time, and I found myself standing being the clique of popular girls the ones with hardly anything on underneath their navy blue caps and gowns. A sense of pride swelled up inside me as I remembered that absolutely nobody had believed in me. Yet here I was, about to prove them all wrong, for the first of many times to come.

I walked across the stage when my name was called, shook hands with every one of my teachers, walked a bit further, stopped and turned toward the crowd before smiling and moving my talisman from one side of the cap to the other. Afterwards, I simply walked off the stage and took my seat. They didn't believe in me, so I did it anyway.

Several other names were called, and I watched as nobody did what I had; for once, it felt nice to be the odd kid out. Then, we were called to stand and hand a rose to our families. I grabbed the three white roses sitting underneath my chair before heading toward my adoptive and foster parents, along with my Auntie Claire and Uncle Thomas. I gave each woman a single white rose before returning to my seat.

None of them had expected this, but it was a formal occasion, and soon I wouldn't have to pretend anymore. Once everyone was back at our seats, we were told to remove but not throw our caps, telling a bunch of teenagers not to do something means they're going to do it anyway.

Collectively, we launched our caps into the air. I laughed and smiled as my mind danced upon the thought that I'd never have to come back again. It was the first step to finding out who I am but the very last taste of my innocence.

Chapter 14

Days after graduation, I'd already moved out of the house and into my first apartment. I had a job as a clerk and the familiar itch for independence. Sadly, my baby brother opted out of attending, and this cut me deeply. He'd been my reason to keep going, but before graduation, we'd gotten into a fight.

I hadn't heard from or seen him in a while, so I made an excuse to visit my folks. When I got there, Dad told me that Noah had started to follow in my footsteps, and my heart began to sink. I didn't want him to end up like me, and I wasn't a good example to follow. So, I decided to find him and have a little chat.

After I was told he was hiding out downstairs, that's where I went. I found him with his back turned, headphones in, blasting heavy metal. He was wearing dark clothing and a jacket at the beginning of summer. My throat tightened upon seeing this because it almost looked like I was staring at my old reflection. I didn't make a noise, but he felt my energy and turned around anyway. I tried to muster a smile as he blankly stared and pulled out one of his earbuds.

"What?"

His tone was sharp and nearly cut like the blades I'd once used to harm myself. I glanced at his arms covered by the jacket and silently prayed he hadn't ever seen those. Biting the inside of my lip, I mustered the strength to say,

"I wanted to see you..."

His deep-sea eyes, once bright and full of life, startled me by how dark they'd gotten, and they grew darker still as he said,

"Well, I don't. Go away. I hate you."

I hate you. I hate you. I hate you. I hate you. I hate you...

Those three words echoed in my head as I felt my heart begin to shatter.

My baby brother, the one person I'd lay down my life for and the only blood I have left, absolutely hated me. Trying to hide the tears in my eyes, I stared down at the grey concrete where I'd once been forced to sleep.

This was the last time I'd be in the same room as my sibling and the very last time I'd ever hear his voice. Afterwards, I began to spiral again, but this time, it got much worse.

Chapter 15

At the time, I had a long-distance boyfriend, and we'd often work on music together. He'd always have some random idea, and I'd come up with lyrics that made better sense. It's actually how we connected and became friends in the beginning.

Strange though, I only remember hearing his voice once or twice. We normally talked over text, and part of me often wondered if he was ashamed of me. This eventually led me to do something I shouldn't have numbing myself out again. Not just with drugs, but alcohol as well. I started to mix things, which led to a partially intoxicated, half-hungover, sickly situation at work. Everyone could tell that I'd probably gotten no sleep and that I was still on something; they were right, the liquor I'd drunk the night before wasn't agreeing with me at all.

I was depressed and struggling to hide it, refusing to talk to my family, but at least I was able to pay my bills before they were due. Then, I lost my job, and the spiral took a bigger and darker turn.

I started contemplating suicide again; standing on the old railway bridge, half drunk and high, I looked down at the raging water and felt my stomach drop to my knees. I'd already written the note, but did I really want to go through with this? Maybe, although I still wasn't sure. It took some mental convincing, but soon I was gripping the rusted metal railing and pulling myself up to stand on the ledge. Every second that I remained standing, the water seemed to become faster and meaner. Then, for some reason, I simply backed off the railing and lay down on the concrete.

Deep sleep washed over me in an instant, and I drifted off on the bridge, right above the raging river. Hours passed by, and eventually, I woke up because of the coldness in the air. I looked around in a daze and noticed that the sky was as black as midnight and guessed that must have been the hour. I had left my phone in the apartment, so I didn't know. Slowly, I got to my feet and started walking away from the bridge. It would take less than twenty minutes to get across town and back to my apartment on foot, and that's exactly what I did. I simply started walking until I stood in front of my own door.

Upon entry, I made a beeline for my phone that'd been connected to the charger and stashed the suicide note in my pocket. There were several missed calls and texts from my parents, along with some from a few local acquaintances, but as usual, absolutely nothing from him.

So, I did something I should've never done and responded to a local guy that I barely knew. He was a tad strange, but I was deeply upset and didn't know what else to do. I'm not sure what had me feeling like I'd been stabbed in the back, but it doesn't exactly matter anymore.

Soon, there was a knock at the door, and I opened it to find Chase, along with his very creepy way of staring at me, standing there with a brown paper sack. He grinned, and I moved out of the way as he waltzed into my apartment. Needless to say, he took something that I probably would've still been able to keep, because just like my Uncle Thomas, I'm not fond of being touched.

After that night, we never spoke again, but I soon discovered that I was pregnant. Talk about instant karma.

I quickly made the choice to keep it and change my ways. Except that's the hard bit, when you don't want help and you kind of suck at communication.

Months passed by in a dense haze, and that didn't stop me from struggling but still figuring things out on my own. By now, my frequent ghoster of a boyfriend still wasn't talking to me, so I blocked his number.

Yes, I'd done something that was wrong, but I'd come to the future realization that the gut feeling of betrayal that led to my behavior had actually been justified. Although, yes, you could say I was technically a harlot back then. I knew people, but I didn't know that these people were never actually my friends.

Chapter 16

It wasn't long until I was in a car, headed back from someplace I shouldn't have been. I wasn't alone, though, there was a young girl named May, with long brunette hair in the driver's seat, and a twenty-something guy named Dave sitting in the passenger seat. His energy was kind of repulsive, but he was helping me back then, or so I thought. He'd claimed to be my baby's father, even though we both knew that wasn't true; it was still a decent gesture. We frequently lived under a false narrative, and it irked me. I still wasn't in contact with my family, not even Paul would say a word to me, and by now, I was eighteen years old.

Everything felt wrong as we began to close the distance to the apartment. Ironically, we had to pass by the Catholic school I'd gone to as a child, and this was when tragedy took hold and I began to pay my karmic debts in full.

An unnerving wave of silent dread began to drench me as we passed by the school, and I got the urge to look out of my window. Sure enough, a large black truck was headed straight for us. My eyes grew wide, and the next several seconds passed by in a blur. The truck hit my door head-on, causing the driver's and my windows to completely shatter. My head hit the back of the driver's seat, and I passed out. May hit the steering wheel and also passed out, while Dave covered his face with his hands and slammed into a faulty passenger-side airbag but remained conscious.

According to him, the car began to fill with smoke from the busted engine, and he panicked after turning to see that both of us had passed out. He unbuckled his and May's seatbelts before bolting to the other side to shake her awake. The first thing she did was start raving about her car that is, until he was able to get her to shut up, get out, and sit along the curbside.

Once again, I was another matter entirely, as usual still unconscious, completely covered in blood, and roughly seven, almost eight months pregnant. We'd just been chatting about my daughter, and I was raving because I wanted to hold her already. I was dreaming about becoming a mom and already planning things out in my head and reality for her.

By now, a group of bystanders had gathered, and it was nearly impossible to get to me. The car had a steadier stream of smoke, and it was apparent to anyone that it might blow at any moment.

Yet, they gathered in fascination to stare at the young, unconscious pregnant girl still sitting in the back. To make it worse, responders wouldn't have been able to open my door anyway, it was completely busted.

It took some shoving, but eventually, the door right behind the passenger side was opened, and my seatbelt was undone. Somebody kept screaming my name and shaking me violently until I slowly started to regain consciousness. Then I was gently led out of the car. Strangely enough, I couldn't see anything that was going on; it was like my eyes were open but everything was simply a darkened haze.

I tried to sit down on the curb that I'd been guided to, but it only resulted in me screaming out in pain; something was very wrong, and the only thing on my mind was my daughter.

I cried out again, and this time someone finally paid attention. They asked a series of stupid questions and shone a light near my eyes, but that was about it. I told them what I knew, which wasn't much, and informed someone that I was close to being able to have my baby. Then, with heavy assistance, I was up off the curb and walking, even though I had no idea where we were headed, and kept commenting on the fact that I still hadn't regained my eyesight.

Again, something danced in my face for a brief second before I was told that I had a concussion.

But what about Illene, my daughter…

Blood kept coming out of me, and I had a dreadful feeling. It felt like an eternity waiting for someone to make the simple decision that required me to go to a hospital. Eventually, Dave piped up and said he'd take me, which I thought was strange, but nonetheless, I allowed myself to be escorted over to a waiting car.

Initially, we did not go to the hospital; he took us straight back to the apartment. This didn't go over well, and after several minutes of arguing back and forth, I forced his hand.

Thankfully, the hospital was only a few blocks away, but upon entry, things got progressively worse. Luckily, my vision had returned before I was rushed into a solitary room, where it felt like they'd made me wait for another eternity.

Finally, the doctor showed and asked the same string of drawn-out questions, but instead of answering them, I opted to get upset and demand that they save my daughter. After some tests were done and scans completed, I passed out only to wake up and hear them say that there was nothing they could've done to save her, and that hit me worse than the black truck had.

Just when I thought my heart couldn't break anymore, it shattered again. I wouldn't be a mother after all. Cursing silently, I felt myself slip back into familiar darkness, but I didn't want anyone to recognize that I'd just given up. After faking several "I'm okay's," I was finally released and told to go home, but in my mind, I'd just lost it.

Chapter 17

A couple of months had passed, and soon it was early November. I made yet another poor decision after bumping into an old high school acquaintance while at work. We didn't keep in touch, and I'd already lost everyone that had been in my life months prior. So, I had no way of knowing if anything had changed.

He also had some rather unique friends who weren't necessarily good influences, but by then, I just wanted to end it without anyone noticing.

However, soon I'd trapped myself in another whirlwind and became the secret in a mess that should've never happened. His name was Dustin, and what I didn't know was that after I'd left, he'd hooked up with one of the popular girls, and she got pregnant. So, he married her.

I had no idea about the marriage, just like I didn't know about the little one. All I knew was what he told me, which was anything but the truth.

At this point, I was the cleaner, clerk, and stocker in a small gas station on the edge of my hometown. He and I lived together. Sometimes he'd try to bring up the past, but I always found a way to avoid those conversations.

There was one day in particular when we were spending it with a friend of his named Gabe, who was a heavy addict. Well, Gabe brought in a small plastic bag of something I'd never seen before in my life, but I acted like I knew what it was. We all ended up drinking pretty heavily, and I got convinced to take a few hits with him.

I instinctively recognized two things: the substance triggered a more prominent connection to the other side, and it would most likely become how I wanted to end things. Of course, neither of these realizations would be spoken out loud, but that night was the start of another addiction that would almost cost my life.

Although fate seemed to have other ideas in store, and less than a month later, I would be driven to a rehab center by one of my old teachers after a bad falling out, where I'd finally learned Dustin had told anything and everything but the truth.

The facility was depressing, but I was more than exhausted, at least for the time being. I stayed there for nearly three weeks until they kicked me out. I still don't understand that bit I'd managed to stay clean for three whole weeks; no obvious desire to relapse, and I'd even begun to try their stupid program. Oh well. They'd also kicked out a few others that day, and some of us began pairing up to handle life on the street. This hadn't happened before, though, and we were addicts, which made the whole ordeal a lot worse.

Those first several days were brutal. We had no idea what to do or how to survive, but eventually, one of us got the bright idea to acquire a phone. After calling someone only they knew, it was relayed that we'd be on the next bus out and headed into a city I'd been to several times. It was near one of my grandparents' homes.

They were strict, German, and kind of odd, but I loved them nonetheless.

Smiling on the inside to be going somewhere at least remotely familiar, I finally took into consideration the fact I didn't have shoes on my feet, and it was nearing the harshest part of Midwestern winter.

I was still eighteen, now homeless, jobless, only three weeks sober, with no shoes on my feet, and no idea if I'd even make it past a few days. A stark contrast to several months prior when I'd had a warm place and the ability to put food on my own table.

Shaking off the dark feeling, I decided to focus on the world around me; it was changing along with my perspective of it. I'd seen darkness before, or so I thought. The events that would soon occur next were something I could've never imagined.

The next couple of days passed by in a blur, and we were in a city I'd previously thought I knew. There was snow on the ground now, and I still had no idea what we were trying to do. I'd also been abandoned. Well, not exactly they'd been arrested, and I'd decided to simply start walking.

I walked for two and a half days across an entire state with little to no sleep or rest don't do drugs, kids. Then I met someone who was also on the street, just in a completely different city, and unlike those who had homes to go to, was surprisingly friendly.

I got scolded for not being dressed properly, but he immediately took me in anyway. I was given a thick woolen blanket, some warm food, and told to rest above the heater vent on the street. After sitting down to eat and sleep, I met a small group of people who were also homeless. One of them asked how long I'd been out, and I had to stop between large bites of pasta and bread to think for a minute before asking,

"What month is it?"

I watched them look at each other before the woman piped up and said,

"It's the last week of November."

I stopped eating like a starving coyote, took a long pull of water, and tried to think back as I said,

"What year is it?"

That got another glance before the same woman answered,

"It's still 2017."

I tried to hide my surprise behind another swig of water, but that only made me cough. I'd graduated high school, got pregnant, lost my baby and my family, then ended up homeless, all within a year and a half flat.

This also meant that I'd be nineteen in a little over six months, if I could make it that long. As well as the fact I'd been on the street for nearly a month and a half now. After realizing I'd been quiet for almost too long, I cleared my throat before commenting,

"It's been nearly three months since I had someplace to go." I looked down after saying that and started picking at the food left in the tin; my hunger greatly subsided by the truth I'd just admitted.

Nobody said anything for a while until one of the men started talking about a church they'd frequently attend. It was a place that surprisingly chose to help street people over everyone else. They often had warm food at the end of every service. I smiled and reflected on every small stop I'd taken; without fail, there'd been a Bible nearby.

Chapter 18

At this point, I had no phone, but nobody was even bothering to look for me anyway. They probably didn't even know that I was gone or cared that I had disappeared. I was living under the overpass, but something often nagged at me that I was far too exposed.

Possibly another week or so passed before I came across a different group that lived in the abandoned freight station along the river. It was far but offered a lot less exposure. However, they had one stipulation: stay sober. So, I did, and it was nice to give up the drugs. Every so often, we'd go to the store, but instead of stealing, we paid with the money we earned performing for people on the street. It was nice; we had our roles and followed street code. We looked out for one another.

However, the group under the bridge had started going heavy on the drugs I'd given up. None of us could blame them, though, it was freezing. We still kept each other clean and continued to earn money by performing for system folks. Very seldom did we stand and hold a sign.

It didn't take a genius to know why: none of us wanted to be on suicide corner, and the cops were unrelenting pricks. Sometimes, in the dead of night, they'd walk up to a street where someone was sleeping, kick them awake, and force them to move. That's not even the worst part they'd take everything away: food, water, clothes, and blankets, all of it. They'd strip us of everything, and we'd be forced to find something better. This only happened to me once, but man, did it suck. They didn't understand and didn't even want to. Sometimes I thought to myself that I wanted nothing more than for one of them to be stranded out here with us.

Most street folks are a lot nicer and more honest than those in the system. They'd give you their very last sack of food if you needed it. Most of the time, systems would scream profanities at us, and some went as far as physical harassment. This is a lesson I picked up rather quickly.

Remember that church I mentioned? Well, I'd go to service every time I could, and it was there that I met another young homeless teenager, around my age. Her name was Jade, and as I got to learn her life story, she told me about her plans to get off the street and that her site was over on the east side.

This was extremely dangerous; folks on that side liked to kill us. They thought of it as a game, and we were the unwilling targets. Well, one night I showed up at service, and she didn't. I had this dark feeling in the pit of my stomach and could hardly focus on anything the Pastor was saying.

He was a rather nice man, and I knew instinctively that he was truly gifted; not one who likes to pretend. It's rare to find someone who teaches in a church that's actually connected to Source. These days, most of them pretend not to sell either. Ask me how I know.

That night after service, the pastor walked up to everyone and shook our hands. When he walked up and shook mine, I got a strange look before he asked softly,

"You're a witch, aren't you?"

I smiled at him, nodded, as I thought to myself,

And you're a real preacher…

I could tell that he wasn't disturbed by that information, and this was rather new to me. Most people tended to behave bitterly, but the word "witch" simply means wise one or connected.

Only when he was done shaking hands did I notice he'd given everyone a five-dollar bill. A rush of warmth enveloped me at his kindness, but immediately afterward, the weight of guilt took its place. I hadn't seen my friend. As everyone turned to begin filing out of the church, I began counting heads; maybe she'd slipped past me or showed up late.

It wasn't until everyone got their hot plates and extra food from the trucks that someone informed the community she'd been killed while leaving her campsite and heading towards the church. A small group of people had snuck behind her, and she'd been beaten to death; all because she was homeless.

Someone screamed, and several people started crying. I felt the wind knocked out of me.

That is not fair.

She had plans and was so close to living a better life. She was someone's child and would've gotten off the street a few days before Christmas. Silently, I gazed up at the pitch-black sky and prayed for her soul to be safe. It was a habit I hadn't done in years.

As an adolescent, I'd been terrified of the dark and would often say my own made-up prayer for protection. It had to be spoken out loud and done every single time I'd be outside or woke up before daylight.

Being on the street brought this back, only slightly different. I was no longer afraid of the dark, and these on-the-fly prayers were no longer for me.

Chapter 19

Soon it was time to celebrate Yule, and after this, the start of another year. Saying there was magic in the air would've been an understatement; everything felt surreal, and I don't remember feeling cold. Of course, the hot chocolate and warm food helped, plus the additional warmers we'd stuffed into our hats, socks, and mittens. I'd been sober since meeting my little group, and it honestly felt wonderful. We'd debated shortly and eventually decided to stand on suicide corner, but not by ourselves. As one would imagine, the cops showed up, but they weren't aggressive with us. Instead, we were given advice, and one of them handed me a bag of food. Seeing this as a day well spent, we waved goodbye to passing cars, and a few screamed,

"Happy Holidays!"

Before helping to gather everything and head toward the depot. Yes, a cop car followed us. Yes, this was rather unnerving mostly because we thought we'd get told to move but instead were informed to stay safe.

That night, I got sick from gorging myself. Even though we had the means to keep it, sometimes old habits die hard. I felt bad for those we'd lost on the street, but I knew they weren't suffering. Sadly, this was my momentary peace before I would be plunged back into darkness.

Days later, we woke up to aggressive banging on the old metal door,

"You've got to move. Leave everything and go. Come on."

I sighed, glancing at my old backpack. It'd once sat in the lockers of every school I'd been in. Now it was hanging from a misshapen hook in an old concrete wall, and I was being told to leave everything behind. Luckily, I didn't have my papers, so I didn't have to worry about losing vital information. That and I'd retained everything to memory; if asked, I could simply recite it and easily be found.

What a way to start a new year, though. The aggressive banging sounded again, and this time I yelled out,

"Give us a fucking minute. We're all still trying to wake up."

We weren't, but they didn't need to know that. I glanced around one final time and nodded towards the couple that had taken me in. They nodded back, and we grabbed our coats, hiding what we could between hats and several layers. Then we filed out the door like nothing had happened. We walked beside each other and down the street until they decided to head in a separate direction. I hugged the woman and shook hands with the man. We didn't say anything, but there wasn't a need.

My very first thought was to obtain food and find somewhere else to go; then somehow I ended up inside a nice, cozy restaurant. I smiled at the staff and asked where the restroom was located, then silently prayed they didn't mistake me for what I used to be. Luckily, they hadn't, and I was pointed in the right direction. Upon entering,

I noticed a rather beautiful woman standing in front of the nest of sinks, and she was intoxicated pretty but drunk.

Immediately, I could tell she wasn't from the street; she had on a rather nice-looking dress and matching scarf. We had a nickname for these types of people, and it wasn't a very pleasant one: dreamer. They have absolutely no idea the system is completely dependent upon them remaining silent and ignorant.

The drunk woman glanced over at me and smiled. I managed a small smile back and moved past her to one of the stalls. I could feel the energy from her, and it was drawing me in. After a few minutes, I unlocked the stall door and stepped out in front of the mirror. She was still standing there, but that wasn't my focus.

I hadn't seen my own reflection in a very long time, and the girl in front of me was anything but a child. Once dull and dark, my eyes were nearly the same shade of blue as my dad's: patchy and blotchy skin, pale as ivory, and my hair had grown longer than it was ever allowed. It framed my face and went past my shoulders in dark auburn waves. I took my own breath away. The only thing I didn't like too much was what I wore, stained dark blue jeans, a poorly patched black winter coat, dirty old boots, and a black beanie. I had forgotten mittens and a scarf to cover my face.

Feeling the heat of eyes watching me, I looked over to find the woman still studying me; she smiled again, but this time I did not return it. Then she said,

"You're beautiful."

This took me off guard because I'd always heard the opposite especially as a child. Glancing down shyly, I nodded a quick thank you and then told her,

"So are you."

This made her grin even wider, and we started talking as if we'd known each other for years. Somehow, I ended up informing her that I was on the street and had been for a while. This caused her to tear up as she told me she'd recently gotten off of them. That struck a chord in me, and I silently vowed if she could do it, then so could I. We spoke for a few more minutes, and then she made me promise something I won't forget.

Her dark green eyes grew serious as she pierced mine,

"Promise me one thing. No matter how bad it gets, and no matter what anyone offers, do not sell yourself. Do you understand? If you do, you can't get out of it."

I knew she wasn't just speaking about physically, so I nodded, but she told me that nodding wasn't going to be enough. So I vocally promised.

Seeming satisfied, we washed our hands and walked out like we were old friends, and she even gave me a hug. She told me that I would be getting off the street someday and to never forget what I'd just agreed upon. I didn't know it then, but it wouldn't be me trying to sell something I shouldn't.

At some point during the day, I'd walked down past the casino and into the open field above the river; it was here that several had made their sites a while ago. I always avoided this place, though, mostly because too many people with the same issues tend to lean towards violent disagreements. Cops didn't come down this way, though, so that was a plus.

Chapter 20

One of the main rules is that it's only proper to announce yourself upon entering someone's site, especially if it's filled with people who'd probably kill you.

So, that's what I did, and the reaction was rather unique. Again, I'd expected to be shown disdain, much like with dreamers, but there weren't any over here. We were all street and one rather large community.

It was recognized quickly that I'd just been kicked, and the next thing I knew, I was handed fresh supplies literally everything I needed and had been forced to leave behind. Pretty soon, I found a spot to set up my site, and a couple folks decided to help. By mid-afternoon, everything was done, and I was starving. Standing and stretching out felt good until I heard a pop and felt sharp pains. Gritting my teeth and sucking in some air, I shifted, snapping my ribcage back into place. It had been like that since the car accident, and every so often, my bones still shift. Saying it hurts is just another understatement. After everything was back into place, I announced I'd be out. Then I left and quickly.

If they found out you had money, they'd kill you, and that's why I booked it so fast. I'd saved up nearly everything from performing on the street, and it was all tucked away in pockets; along with my favorite knife and a folded note with identification written on it in case my body was ever found. It had everything from my name to the childhood home address and numbers to call.

Unfortunately, the local and not-so-local dreamers were rather rude that day, and I found myself praying a few of them ended up outside with me.

I just couldn't seem to catch a break. After biting back my tongue to the point I thought it might fall off, I ran back out onto the street with bags of food I'd just bought. There were enough supplies in my hands for over a month if I rationed right. Then it hit me: I couldn't just walk back carrying this. It was a clear message that somehow I'd gotten a hold of some nice change. So, I took off one of my jackets and began moving everything over.

When it looked decent, I started again, and upon walking back in, asked if anyone needed something. A couple folks piped up, and we sat down to exchange. Everything worked out perfectly, and by now it was nearing nightfall.

More people began filing back in from a day of going about their merry business, and I gathered what was left to move back over to my site. It wasn't much, but at least it was better than nothing. I had a six-person tent, clothes, food, water, woolen blankets, and a warm sleeping bag.

However, during the time I was rearranging, I felt someone staring and turned to lock eyes with a guy I should've stayed far away from. He stared and smiled, but it never reached his dark eyes. He was tall, well dressed, and eerily healthy for someone who claimed to be on the street. Something about him felt off, but that didn't seem to stop the pull of energy.

Part of me still hates admitting to it, but I didn't exactly care. He had striking dark and mixed features and seemed to be waiting on me. Not wanting to seem rude, I turned and came out of my site. The entire time, he stared and waited. Then when he spoke, I knew exactly what he was, but I didn't want to say it.

The conversation seemed to flow rather quickly, and I found myself being led out of the community. There were no thoughts running through my mind; I simply walked beside him, looking into his eyes the entire time. We continued to speak even as we helped each other climb into an abandoned church. The ground wasn't hollow; it had long turned sour, and before much time had passed, I lost all sense of time.

I'd started using it again, but by now it was much worse. I was bordering on complete dependency, and the other two in the church were my suppliers, literally.

Chapter 21

At some point, we came across others, and one of them had a car. It was a run-down piece of junk but still ran. Although, I can't say I trusted any of them; even with the addiction confiscating my intuition and overpowering many things.

We had a long discussion and concluded that none of us wanted to remain in the church forever. It was condemned and probably already scheduled for demolition. Since none of us wanted to stay where we were, thoughts of traveling became quite attractive, and for that, we would need a car.

A couple of days passed, and then I found myself wrapped in blankets, riding four deep, sitting near another person I didn't know. I was high. Hell, we all were, aside from the one sitting next to me, which was rather suspicious to the driver; I didn't really care.

I sat behind the guy who'd been waiting outside my site, and occasionally he reached behind him to make sure I was still there. Sometimes I caught him staring at me through the reflection of the passenger mirror. Soon enough, though, the lull of the car pulled me into a deep sleep.

I slept for hours until I was woken up and told to get food. It hadn't occurred to me then that there were only three of us now until I witnessed a gun exchange hands and heard that trust had been obtained. A few more hours went by, and I found myself asleep once again. That was the downside of being an addict: if you didn't use for a certain amount of time, withdrawals started, and the first thing you wanted to do was sleep.

Then, as if given an unexpected ice shower, I woke to find that we were outside a row of apartments. They appeared to be small, and I quickly followed the other two across the street until a church next to them caught my eye, and I found myself coming up with an excuse.

The guy from that night immediately caught on to what I was thinking, and we headed over, barely registering that his companion nodded or that he had already entered the apartment. We walked inside, and I felt the same peace I had as a child so many years ago.

Interestingly enough, the one who came with me seemed uncomfortable, but right before he could turn us around to leave, a pastor walked out. He had a warm smile and bright, dazzling eyes; his energy felt very welcoming. As he looked from me to my companion, I noticed a flash of heat from his frequency field a very telling hint about the information he'd just mentally received. This is something I know a little too well, as energy is sort of my thing.

He asked our names, and my companion gave a poorly executed storyline. The pastor nodded and asked if we were thirsty. I agreed. Then he turned and went to get us each water upon his own initiative. I stood patiently while the other did not; he kept pacing and playing with his clothing.

I knew something was very wrong but didn't want to mention it. After the pastor returned, he gave us each a bottle of water. I shook his hand and thanked him as the second companion opened the door behind us.

"So this is where you two lovebirds went? Come on. Let's go."

I could tell neither of them was comfortable being around an active church, but I didn't quite understand why. I waved and smiled at the pastor before following them both back across the street to the apartments.

Upon entry, there was a woman who seemed very out of place, her energy was dark, as were the other people in the house.

I noticed pretty quickly there were more men than women and instinctively opted to be close to the door. Something wasn't right. One of the companions went into the back bedroom where most of the men were; they had been staring at me from the minute we walked in. This left me, the woman, and the second companion together in the front room.

She kept trying to get us to give up our real names, but something told me not to, and I was grateful that every time she asked, he insisted on answering for me. She obviously didn't believe a word about where we'd come from, but was smart not to press.

By now, I had a dark and sinister feeling twisting in the pit of my stomach. I knew I had to run but wasn't sure when. It was just this near-overwhelming feeling that kept gnawing at me. However, I shortly got my answer as the back bedroom door opened and several pairs of strange beady eyes peered out at me. They were only interested in me, and as they continued to watch my every move, I noticed every gaze had a glossed-over, demon-like reflection. I saw one of them smile at me, and the companion I'd been sitting next to leaned over.

Carefully and in a very hushed tone, he told me,

"You need to run but only when I tell you. Don't try to grab anything. Just go. If I'm not right beside you, I'll meet you."

I nodded slowly at his words and glanced from the sea of beady glass eyes toward the extremely confused woman in front of an old computer. I was very glad he hadn't given my real name at that moment, as he was the only one who knew it. Otherwise, things would have gone much differently. We both watched as the woman was called into the room and the door shut behind her. Then he nodded at me, and I took off out the front door. Soon, he kept pace alongside me, and we were gone. That dark void-like feeling hadn't lessened, but at least the sun was warm.

We alternated running and walking for what felt like several days with absolutely no breaks. I knew what they wanted wasn't good and, at one point, tried to flag down an officer; but that didn't go well as we quickly realized he was part of it.

Everywhere we turned, somebody had placed food, water, drugs, or cash; it was all a game to them a very dangerous one. If he'd picked up one of the latter items, I'd be gone in an instant, and vice versa. This went on until we chose to stand in front of the federal building, mostly because we were tired and knew it had audio/video recording cameras on at all times. That was also my mom, Lyann's, place of employment.

It didn't take long before somebody across the street aimed a six-shot revolver at my head, and I heard the familiar click as they moved the chamber. Still, I didn't move even as the growing light illuminated people crouched behind brush and near trees, close enough to almost touch me. It was the same people from the apartment, still playing sick games.

We remained standing in front of the building until two federal employees told us to move. However, moving didn't last long as my vision went black and my legs gave out underneath me. This would end up being our way out but my direct path into a brand-new problem that almost cost me my life.

We ended up being sent to the nearest hospital, and my companion spoke for me the entire time. He quickly told the staff a story about how we'd recently gotten married, tricked by traffickers, and that something was wrong. He spun quite the tale, and soon we were placed inside a room and told nobody except staff would have access to us.

Then the doctor came in, and so did some cops. They started asking questions. I watched him alternate between the truth and painting pictures. Afterwards, they turned and started questioning about the drugs found in my system. Fuck. I'd forgotten I was still coming down. That's when we caught each other's eye, and I saw something click.

He told them we'd been drugged, which wasn't exactly untrue. They asked for names, and we hesitated at first but eventually gave up street names and real identities. After the cops and doctor left, we shared a sigh of relief, and I watched him truly grin for the first time in a while. He laughed and took my hand before saying,

"Now all we have to do is wait. We just bought ourselves some time, babe."

I knew it wasn't real but felt happiness swell nonetheless. He was acting but had still willingly taken a risk for me.

Pretty soon, we were laughing as we recounted that morning's latest feat we'd discovered the bridge was still under construction and the only way to walk across was by using a single beam of plywood. He'd dashed over first, nearly fell, then held it steady so I could scurry across. Crazy, considering I'm afraid of heights, but some measures had to be taken.

Chapter 22

We stayed in the hospital for nearly a week until I regained some ability to use my legs again. I was still weak, but there wasn't much choice. They had found us, and some of them were already in the building.

A kind woman who had been my nurse booked us a ride to another state and helped plan our escape route. She wanted us safe. However, temporarily and the only way to do that was to leave. Shoes were thrown on feet as quickly as papers exchanged hands. He thanked her, and they both helped me from a wheelchair into a waiting car.

I hung my head low, pulling the hood of my sweatshirt over my face, and blamed myself. Even temporarily, losing the use of your legs out here was suicide. That was dangerous and could have ended badly. Soon, though, the car stopped in front of the station, and he hurried to help me stand on my feet. We walked hand in hand, keeping our eyes shifting across the crowd. After getting on the bus, we sat in the far back; he took the aisle seat and gave me the window a protective gesture. We rode for what was probably hours, occasionally exchanging a handful of comments. It quickly became apparent the driver was a prick; he didn't do breaks and had actually left someone running after the bus when they asked to stop and use the restroom. I was grateful, though, because fewer stops meant less risk. I passed the time people-watching and playing the games Dad and I had grown up with.

At some point, I dozed off and was woken up by hearing our stop was next. A different state. A different city. Similar landscape. No sooner had we gotten off the bus than we came face to face with another street kid. He was roughly our age and had ill intentions written all over him, but for an hour or so, we decided to humor him before running off again. That's when the two of us crossed paths with a man who would soon teach me some very painful life lessons.

He was tall and handsome, much older than me or my companion, with deep chocolate brown eyes and striking indigenous features. He only gave a street name, but I'd later learn his real name was Tyler, and he asked if we needed assistance.

That's when we exchanged stories and learned he was also from the street. This took me by surprise, considering he looked well-fed and nicely groomed. Inwardly, I smiled, of course, he would take pride in himself. Much to my companion's growing dislike, I felt drawn to him. Soon, he invited us to his site, and we walked for a good couple of minutes. Once again, I was happily shocked at his craftsmanship; he'd managed to build a small home out of half-decent wooden planks. He'd also set up a protection system in case someone unwelcome showed up. This was impressive.

He invited us inside, but as we continued our discussion, a knock came at the door they were kicking him out. I felt bad, almost like it was our fault, but we took what could be taken and decided to hide the rest. Thankfully, they had given us all the time we needed, but we didn't need much. Everything shifted between hands swiftly, and soon we filed out to shocked workers.

He nodded and even thanked them before leading us to the overpass on the other side of the road. It took a couple of weeks, but eventually, we got into a rather common routine.

Initially, neither of us wanted to tell him that I had recently regained the use of my legs, but given the circumstances, we didn't have much choice. He freaked out and got mad at my companion. It was either the beginning or middle of spring by then I wasn't sure which; either way, it was almost constantly raining. All I was aware of was that we'd gotten hooked on the same thing again, just in a different state this time.

I hated myself for it.

Several more weeks went by, then my companion and I got into a drug-induced argument with our acquaintance. It was bad, and we ended up leaving for a few days. The entire time, it never stopped raining.

Both of us became hungry, tired, cold, and sober a bad mix. Even though we'd been through a lot together, this put a strain on our connection, and I began to feel him shift elsewhere. Luckily for me, after another night of freezing and half-hiding from the rain, I convinced him to go back. To say I was tired of everything would have been an understatement.

Once again, we were welcomed, but this time we all set some ground rules; the first was to keep each other clean. I readily agreed, but it took some convincing for him. After this, we settled into another routine that lasted about three weeks. Then I got into an altercation with my companion and left with Tyler.

Silently, I hoped he would stop me, but he didn't, and soon he completely vanished from my life. Sometimes I reread the note he left, and among several things, he kept repeating that he wasn't angry and hoped I'd find whatever it was I had been searching for even though I had no idea what that was.

My heart grew colder as I broke our vow to each other. We wouldn't be in each other's lives, so what was the point? A lot of things kept me fending: the loss of my daughter, nobody caring enough to come look, life not being what I'd expected.

In short, I sort of slipped between the cracks of depression, suicidal thoughts, and just wanting someone to do it for me. Then an opportunity came that accentuated the darkness in the perfectly timed play known as my life.

Chapter 23

We'd been at a gas station, and I had gone inside to get us some food. As I was walking out, there was a big smile on my face. I'm not sure why, but I felt warm inside. It might have had something to do with the kind dreamer behind the counter or that today just seemed beautiful. For some reason, he didn't like it, and I could tell by the darkened look in his eyes. After thanking the nice kid, I walked out the door, still smiling, and headed over to him with a small bag of food.

That's when he hit me for the first time. I dropped everything as my nose broke, and blood started pouring from between my fingers. All he did was glare and clench his fist.

"Why the hell are you smiling?"

I looked at him, confused, and gave a blank-minded answer. His eyes grew darker, and he hit me again. From the corner of my bruising right eye, I watched a light blue car pull up. The group inside started laughing as they witnessed violence in front of them.

I watched him wave his hand toward them, and instantly they fell silent. He had pull and respect; I didn't. He then told me to pick up what had been dropped and started walking away. Hurriedly, confused, and very much in pain, I did as instructed, still wondering what had happened. I replayed old conversations we'd had late at night, where he'd confessed to being a felon, and we'd talked about how life hadn't turned out how he thought it would.

We also talked about his old ambitions and how much he'd once loved to dance. He told me stories and secrets that I'll take to my grave because his story is not mine to tell.

Unfortunately, he quickly discovered that I responded to violence and set out to teach me some things in the wrong manner. Now, daily occurrences shifted once again. Some days were good, and on others, I'd soon be covered in my own blood.

He hated the smell of blood, and every time I did something wrong, he always asked the same question:

"Why do you make me do this?"

I always racked my brain for an answer but could never find one, and by now, I had become entirely dependent on the drug to keep the pain away.

Days flashed by in a blur, and soon we found ourselves in the middle of summer. Most days were scorching, and I couldn't show my face because it was covered in blood and bruises. Then, we made a deal.

It was nearing my birthday, and I honestly don't think he was very fond of hitting me. I know how crazy that sounds, but bear with me. We both wanted something, so the deal was simply to pay attention to what he was trying to do and go a certain amount of time without pissing him off.

He admitted to having forgotten what I looked like without bruises, and I honestly had as well.

My consecutive record of days without getting hit? Turned out to be exactly fourteen. I screwed up on my birthday and got beat for it, badly.

It started out wrong almost immediately. Everything felt off, but we both tried to ignore it. After all, it was my birthday. However, I couldn't shake what I had just witnessed from my vision.

There had been a warm feeling and then pictures of a familiar woman. She was beautiful, with dark flowing hair and similar features to my own. These flashes came through as if on a screen, and then I heard a quiet feminine voice whisper,

I'm sorry I couldn't protect you, but I never meant to hurt you. I thought you would be safe. Please forgive me, sweetheart. I'm so sorry.

Then, as quickly as it had arrived, it vanished, and I woke up to being told he had a surprise waiting. This made my stomach drop, even as a knock sounded from outside our site. He flashed a smile, then opened the entrance, revealing a small group of people who quickly came inside.

We all sat around talking, and eventually, it was mentioned that it was my birthday. Of course, this hadn't come from me. The next instant, a blade was passed to him, and then to me. I smiled and nodded a quick thanks. The first gift I'd received in a long time. It was beautiful, small, and my favorite shade of violet. Almost as soon as they'd come, he sent them away, and we headed out of our site.

We walked down the street toward the gas station to get food. Then it was off to the trailer park, where things would go south rather quickly.

He knew people who lived there, and none of them were upstanding. Then again, neither were we.

Even as the twisting feeling in my gut grew, I followed him toward one of their homes. Before too long, we were sitting around a small table talking. He told his friend it was my birthday and asked how old I was; I'd just turned twenty-one.

Apparently, this was funny because I was finally allowed to drink. I'd drunk before legal age but didn't mention this to either of them and hadn't touched a drop since before ending up on the street. His friend mixed some drinks, and I ended up downing mine; he didn't like that too much.

I occasionally caught him glaring at me, and soon I'd done something that set him off. He ran out the door, and I quickly apologized to his friend before heading after him. My stomach began twisting tighter, and the dark feeling grew.

He was walking away.

Confused, I started to follow. He screamed for me to go back to his friend, but I blatantly refused, still unsure what I'd done. Soon, he stopped walking altogether and waited until I caught up.

That's because we were finally out of eyesight. He didn't even turn as an explosion of pain erupted. My nose broke once again, and fresh bruises began to swell where I'd been struck. At some point, I'd fallen to the ground, but he didn't stop. He began to kick me and demand that I stand up. Instead, I curled into a ball, intent on protecting myself as much as possible.

I still don't know how long it went on, but I was grateful when he finally stopped. He told me to quit covering and stand, then reprimanded me and said he was ashamed to lay hands on me again. He had been proud of me, and until then, he'd been able to see my face and eyes. I knew he didn't like hurting me, and as he began to walk away again, I followed. He stopped near the train tracks, turned, then said,

"Don't follow me. You know I don't like when you do that. Now, come here. I know you were taught differently, but we're equals. Stand and walk beside me."

He ushered me to stand by his side, and hesitantly, I did so. Tyler was right, and it instantly felt very foreign. I glanced anxiously from the treeline down the tracks until he tilted his head to block my vision,

"Do you think I enjoy hurting you?"

His eyes held so much pain that I had to shift my head and look toward my feet as he continued,

"I'd give everything up not to hurt you, but you only seem to respond to pain, and it's the only thing I know. I've told you about my past. You know me better than anyone. I'm trying to teach you, but this is the only way either of us understands."

Only, I didn't understand back then, and it wouldn't be until a few years later that it all finally clicked.

We walked side by side down the tracks until it was time to branch off and head back to our site. I was grateful for the nightfall because it helped hide the bruises, but I was unaware that in a few days, exactly on his birthday, something else would cause another fight between us, and we'd never meet again.

Chapter 24

The next six days passed by in a blur of blood, pain, fighting, drugs, and depression. Then, a thought I had a few months back came to fruition. I had wished for death.

It was around dusk when either of us woke, and the day was already spent; we had nothing to show for it, and he immediately had a foul mood.

He kept complaining about the bruises on my face. I think he hated himself for it.

I kept my head down as he headed out to lift his weights; we often worked out together. Soon, he called me to come out and join him; against the twisting in my stomach, I did so.

He'd set up little planks of wood along the base of a concrete wall, then told me to break them. I was immediately confused. So, he demonstrated by kicking one of them with his foot, and I watched it splinter into three different pieces. I looked at him as he gestured for me to follow suit. Except when I tried, it didn't splinter; instead, my foot bounced right off. Thinking I had pissed him off, I moved away quickly, but he just laughed and smiled before saying,

"You're doing it wrong. Tell yourself it's already broken. Then try again."

I nodded at his words and tried again; this time it snapped into two pieces, and I looked up at him grinning wildly. In his eyes, there was pride, and we spent the remaining sunset working out together.

I'm not sure how it started, but once again I'd done something wrong. The argument got to the point I threatened to leave and turned away. He kicked me from behind, and I fell face down in red dirt. He told me to get inside, and without much thought, I did so. This made him even angrier; he not only trashed the site but continued to lay hands on me, sometimes saying,

"You just do whatever you're told, huh? What if I said to go kill yourself? Would you fucking do it?"

He had a valid point, but I didn't understand. I'd been raised to hardly make a sound, and he didn't like that. I was taught to be part of a system without complaining. These were the traits he hated so much, but it would take a few years to finally understand.

Soon, he told me he would be going for a walk and not to follow. I knew from my birthday what might happen if I did, so after he left, I started trying to fix everything that had been broken. Unbeknownst to me, this was something else I did wrong.

Several minutes passed, and by the time he returned, darkness had long fallen. He found me still trying to fix something and set off into another rage. It got physical again, and soon he'd picked up a bat, hitting me across the stomach and both legs repeatedly. Large bruises quickly swelled, but I couldn't feel anything thanks to excessive nerve damage.

I wasn't able to protect myself, and soon a wave of red-hot heat washed over me from a freshly broken arm. The next thing I knew, I was screaming, and he simply stopped.

There were no more beatings.

I watched as his eyes went from pitch black to soft brown and filled to the brim with fear. He looked at my arm, clenched tightly to my chest, muttered something, and bolted. I had no idea where he was headed or if he'd come back. All I knew was pain.

He'd snapped my bone as easily as he'd taught me to break those planks. It took a few minutes, but finally, I recognized the sound of approaching sirens, and by now, he'd returned. He was breathless and kept demanding that I didn't go into shock; then he tried picking me up, and I screamed. I started feeling extremely cold, which was odd for the middle of summer, but soon he'd placed me into an empty cart and covered me with a large wool blanket. Then he ran like hell to meet responders.

When we arrived, they haphazardly pulled me from the cart, and I screamed once again. The pain was the one thing I tried focusing on. I watched one of them turn and ask what happened, catching the fear in his eyes as he watched me being placed into the ambulance. I could tell he didn't want to go back as he recounted the false story he'd told me to say whenever someone asked.

I still don't think the responder was dumb enough to believe him, but smart enough not to press. He asked where I was going, and without fail, one of them lied straight to his face. He was told a different hospital than the one I would be taken to, and by the time we got there, my arm was already set in a makeshift cast. I was met by a team of doctors, nurses, and cops, but I couldn't stop myself from looking for Tyler. They tried to ask what happened, and without fail, I told the same lie he had.

I know it's a form of perjury, but fear will do that to a person. Luckily, they didn't question it, and soon I was moved into my own room where a real cast would be placed on my arm within minutes.

It was quickly brought to my attention that I weighed no more than eighty pounds and was completely covered in blood, bruises, and dirt. That's when I broke down. Part of me wanted to reach out and contact my parents, but then I remembered that none of them had bothered to find me.

So when they asked for my name, I told a partial lie and gave the one I'd had at birth. Technically, it's still my name but hasn't been used since late 2006 or '07.

In my eyes, there must have been a lot of pain, but they probably thought it was because of something else.

A few days passed, and I was informed there was no place for me to go. They'd have no choice but to send me back onto the street. That's when quick thinking and guilt took me by surprise, and I pulled a nurse aside to tell the truth. A doctor was told, and police responded once again. It was the same officer; he didn't say much other than,

"So you're finally ready to tell us what really happened? Why don't you go ahead and get started."

Instantly, he made me think of my dad, who'd been an officer growing up and had told me stories about cases he'd worked on. Most of them were horrifying, and that's why he'd taken to teaching me how to fight.

I nodded and recounted that night.

He took several notes, and afterwards asked to take photos of the bruises.

I said he could before receiving his card. After thanking him and watching as he left, I peered out the window to the busy street below.

If they put me back out there, he'd know about it before nightfall, and I don't think he'd be so forgiving.

Much like the woman before me, he'd sent her to the hospital with strict instructions not to return to the street; she did so anyway. He found out about it, and that's all I'm going to say.

I didn't want to be back out there, so when the next nurse came in, I asked her to help me. She said she'd do everything she could, and before lunchtime, I was on the phone making arrangements. It would be in a small town, but I'd have enough time to recover and figure out everything that happened while I was gone maybe even meet a few interesting people.

After going through intake, I was given clothes and some other items. It was a place people would run to when they didn't want to die. One of the staff showed me where I'd be staying, and then I slept for an entire month. It was the best sleep I'd had in forever, and unfortunately, it was the only restful one for a while.

Upon waking, my mission was food. I made my way into the kitchen, feeling extremely dizzy and disoriented due to lack of nutrients for Divine knows how long. Thanks to past events, I knew I had to eat slowly and in small portions. So, I made a peanut butter sandwich with a glass of milk and an orange simple but the best meal I'd had in forever. Afterwards, I glanced at the back door: it was fenced in, and there were cameras everywhere, but I was still worried.

That lasted about a week, then I was outside anytime I could. At one point, someone gave me an iPad, and I snooped when I wasn't listening to music. I found out that my grandmother Rose had passed away, my first love had gotten with the girl he claimed was just a friend, my little brother was being an idiot, and a couple of other things.

I'd already known she'd passed, but what struck me was the fact he got with the girl he claimed was a friend. I did the math, and it added up to foul play. He'd been dating both of us at the exact same time and, after I disappeared, made his choice. I was sad for about five minutes, then went back to snooping.

You can't change the past.

A couple of months went by, and it was nearing Yule again. I was being told they might send me back outside. That's something I wouldn't allow to happen, so after some encouragement from one of the girls, I finally reached out to my family.

A few days later, my dad showed up, armed and ready with a long road trip rant. I was silently grateful I hadn't called him from the hospital no child wants their parents or anyone to see them that way.

However, I was still given the third degree the entire time, and all it did was make me feel worse. Dad didn't want to understand; he just wanted to treat me like a child. He brought up some things from the past, and I found myself biting back both tears and my sharp tongue.

They'd never taken kindly to how I handled my depression. At one point during my adolescence, I'd been handed a knife and told not to get blood in the house when I killed myself. This brewed to the point my baby brother unknowingly stopped me. But when I ended up in the psych ward because of them, they still didn't stop.

I didn't mention any of this, though, and soon found myself dissociating.

As I looked out the truck window, something inside me snapped, and I finally realized these people were never my family.

Your family doesn't drive you to suicide, push you into addiction, push you to your limits, and then blame you for everything.

I sighed heavily before partially turning back into the conversation and saying,

"So you're telling me I'm not welcome back."

He nodded in agreement before continuing,

"That's right, you're not welcome, but what we can do is put you back up in your own apartment again. I'll stop by every day or every other day. Keep it clean. Get a job. Maybe we can work together. How does that sound?"

Internally, I was rolling my eyes, but externally, I kept a straight face and responded,

"Sure, Dad. Sounds like a plan."

Although I knew he meant the best, it still stung. Soon, he started asking what happened, but I didn't have the energy to explain anything.

After several hours filled with silence, we started passing familiar ground; crossing close to the same bridge I'd almost jumped from as a teenager.

We stopped at a cafe on the other side to eat, and my appetite did not go unnoticed. I ate everything and then told him I was still hungry. He laughed and gave me what was left of his. I avoided eye contact as I shoved more food in my face.

That's until he told me there would probably be an apartment I could sleep in that night. I looked up from devouring crispy bacon and hash browns. That was fast. After we finished, it was back to the car and down to the other side of town. There was, in fact, an apartment. I slept on the floor, and the next day, Dad took me to the main building.

The landlady had been somewhat briefed. She gave me an apartment and a job. Then they laid out rules you'd probably hear for a teenager. It wasn't an issue for me, though; I'd already been planning to stay sober and far away from people. Soon enough, it was the end of another year, and I felt very proud of myself. I was off the street, sober, and physically healing decently. I even worked where I lived. So much had happened for me in such little time.

True to their word, I wasn't allowed on the farm. And since I don't typically celebrate holidays, it worked out fine. The nightmares were brutal, though. Every night, I had the same death dream: he stood over me, and the beatings didn't stop until I stopped screaming. His eyes were two pitch-black orbs as he wore an expression laced with pure malice. The same words echoed through my brain:

Why do you make me do this?

At some point, those nightmares struck a nerve and began turning into something else entirely. We switched places, and this time, I didn't stop until he quit moving. The rage I felt was nearly overpowering, and it scared me. That's never been who I am, though, and I didn't want to hurt him.

Instead, I wanted to understand.

Chapter 25

Seamlessly, I fell into another routine and even began to have an inside joke with my dad. Eventually, I convinced myself to get a second job, and it turned out to be a very bad idea.

I almost went back into some old patterns before getting my shit together; yes, somehow I was still a bit naive and allowed a problem to move himself into my apartment. This problem didn't work, didn't clean, drank alcohol, did drugs, tried to get me to relapse, and had a bunch of people around that I didn't know; basically broke every rule there was and then some.

They'd often keep me awake for hours, and it got so bad I was asked a few times if I'd relapsed. Oh, and he never paid rent or helped with any of my bills. So when I found out what he'd been doing behind my back, I was more than glad to kick him out.

After exterminating the mess I'd willingly allowed into my life, it got a bit easier; for a little while at least. I started Livestreaming when I wasn't working and had a nice small group of friends who all seemed to have the audacity to live miles away from me. Can you imagine that?

It wasn't much, but it was fun. Sometimes I'd do readings for people who asked, and sometimes I'd just be bored. I did whatever I could to avoid the inevitable realization that I was still severely depressed; I even tried ignoring the nagging feeling that my current situation was superficial, though I knew nobody in my family could be trusted.

So, I began to focus more on the strong pull I'd always felt from another dimension; aside from my grandmother's secret teachings, I'd never explored it myself.

Except this was different, and soon I began burning dragon's blood; it wouldn't be until a few years later that I learned Lady Lilith had been reaching out to assist me. Life was quiet, simple, very mundane, and very much not me. There were still lessons that I needed to learn, and against the growing desires of those near me, I decided to go learn them.

My biggest lessons turned out to be from a scrawny guy who should've been left talking to himself in my unseen messages. He showed up, after being asked not to, and spent the next few days in my apartment.

I had been given and bought some rather nice things, and it should've been a deal breaker that he'd talked down about my folks, but I wasn't mature enough to realize that. Then within less than a week, life took a 180 down the drain. I went from being at the top of my game to completely isolated and emotionally destroyed.

I'm not sure why I stayed as long as I did, perhaps it was due to shame. We moved almost as fast as one could blink, and at first I hung onto every word he said; that's until he called the cops and broke my phone after catching me talking to relatives all because I wanted to leave; dishes were thrown, holes were punched into walls, and anything you could think of, I bore witness. It got a bit concerning when I went to pack my backpack and told him I would be leaving. He'd slid in front of the door, held up a knife, and practically demanded,

"You're not going anywhere."

Immediately memories came rushing back, and all I wanted to do was leave. I pushed him aside and unlocked the door; unfortunately, he'd followed me, blocking the exit, and showed he was already on the phone with dispatchers. Needless to say, he lied his ass off to the dispatcher while still holding a knife aimed my way. His plot didn't work because she heard me mutter,

"Stop blocking the door and let me leave please. I just want to go home."

Responders arrived after I'd already dissociated, and he began spinning his tale; then one of them pulled me aside and asked if I felt safe. I didn't hesitate to tell them that I didn't. They offered to grab my papers, and I left for a few months.

Wasn't long until I finally noticed the bruises he'd left on me. This deeply bothered me because it showed what I'd allowed to happen again. I was a punching bag, but of course this notion wouldn't be completely accepted until a few years down the road when I finally had enough.

It didn't take long after I left for him to claim he would change, but how are you gonna change your ways if you're knee-deep inside the next-door neighbor? He didn't know that I knew, but soon I would sadly go back in enough time for my twenty-second birthday, which would be ruined because another woman's wants were deemed more important.

Supposedly, she was just a friend of his, and she was married to a rather nice man. I'd woken up that day to them talking on the phone about what she wanted to do, and none of it sounded like any fun to me.

Nobody cared to listen though, aside from her husband, who hadn't even known it was my birthday. He ended up being my only real friend during that time. Shockingly, I'd managed to stay sober but I'd still turned to an old habit: self-harm.

I was extremely suicidal, and the lack of food didn't help either. We barely had anything, and when we did, it never lasted long. One thing led to another, and soon I almost let him walk me back down to the streets; the only thing I'll avoid like the plague, aside from people.

It wasn't all bad though; I'd ended up getting a job at the coffee shop down the street from where we were staying. It was catty corner to a tattoo place where I ended up getting most of my ink done.

By now, I was twenty-three and both emotionally and mentally checked out but wasn't sure what else to do. So, I let him do whatever he wanted and went about my business.

It was fun, making coffee for people, getting to know their likes and dislikes; I learned a lot about myself through journaling, meditation, and self-reflection. Sometimes I miss the shop, its bright atmosphere, and the people who pushed me to keep pursuing my passions for both modeling and writing; everyone who worked there was some form of neurologically diverse, and it was nice not to be judged.

Especially when one of my coworkers caught me dancing to stay awake during the early morning shift. I dance a lot like my dad, and he's got two left feet, but at least there's enthusiasm. These bright days wouldn't last forever, and soon I was being told we had no place to go; I was also graduating on the same day they kicked us out.

Which turned into a bittersweet moment that foreshadowed a lot more goodbyes.

Soon, we moved into a house filled with people that didn't exactly like me; it felt like being controlled again. Especially because they didn't like that I'd gotten much further into my practice; for some reason, it made them extremely uncomfortable to learn that I've practiced for years and that I'm a natural born.

At one point, I was begged to attend a church because they thought it would help cleanse me. Part of me still wonders how they would've reacted to learning that I was doing the same thing as their preachers, only in a much more direct manner. I'm simply traveling along a path that involves pretty cards, Latin words, the light of the moon, and sometimes their holy book. I'm very much used to the hostility though.

By now, I was twenty-four and already knew he'd been messing around again. So, I prepared to completely detach. After sleepless nights spent wondering how I could get him to expose himself, a rather unique thought came to me: I could ask for it to happen. So, I did. I asked for a mistake to be made similar to one he'd already made; shortly after my request, it was accepted, and he made a very foolish mistake indeed.

However, I wouldn't just catch him. He'd actually admitted to it and made it seem as if it was my fault entirely.

He pulled into the drive after another supposed long night of tagging unregistered vehicles and hoped to see me sound asleep. I was wide awake. After flashing a quick smile at me, I caught sight of his phone screen, and it wasn't the same background as before.

There was a much younger half-naked girl standing in front of a bathroom mirror wearing one of my dad's shirts. It'd been the one he gave me because of my panic attacks and he didn't want it anymore. I often wore it every single time I missed home. Now I knew where it had gone.

Anger boiled in my blood as I glared at him silently, and I watched his eyes go from joyful to scare. He began to stutter and tried to explain,

"It's not what it looks like, I swear. It's just a joke, see?"

He opened his phone and returned the background to a recent picture of us at one of my favorite band's concerts, but I wasn't convinced. My heart grew cold as I took the engagement ring off and tried to hand it back to him,

"Since you refused to stay loyal, give it to her."

It got heated, and he threw a temper tantrum; I had a not-so-bright moment myself and ended up exposing him as a liar and a cheat to his entire family. His parents had to separate us after he tried to push me down the stairs.

I went back into the room and finally broke down in tears while he went downstairs to call her. I stayed in that room for days and just cried my eyes out. No matter how prepared I was, it still hurt; almost like a red-hot poker being repeatedly stabbed into the same area. After a few days and some words of encouragement from his dad, I began picking myself up again.

I started deleting photos and made plans with a distant friend to move away so I could start over. I knew staying wasn't going to help, and I rather liked meeting new people. Finally, we arranged a date, and I started to close off my heart to everything and everyone.

When it came to the day, he tried to cause me to stay. This went from leaving late to asking for a final hug with tears in his eyes. There was even a suggestion to remain in contact, but he was already on my blocked list.

I fell asleep on the plane and ended up having one of those freefall dreams. Something unexpected was going to happen and fast. I mentally began preparing for anything but never imagined things would turn out quite like they did.

Before the plane landed, I remembered an artist that he'd gotten rather upset with a year or so back; now it made me laugh but then it had been bothersome.

I'd wanted a new tattoo, just line work, and against my silent wishes, he opted to stay for the entire process. Not only was he intoxicated, but he'd taken hits of some things I wanted nothing to do with.

The artist kept getting frustrated because my ex would walk around all strangely, and at one point, the artist threatened to steal me from him. I actually thought about letting him; he was older and a lot more my type.

That pissed my ex off, and after everything was done, he said I'd never be going back. A few months later, he conveniently found a different artist, who was a lot quieter but still more my type than he ever was.

Right as the plane landed, my phone rang, and I glanced down to see it was my friend calling. As we filed off, I had no idea that my patience was about to be tested, and over the next couple of weeks, everything would dramatically change.

It was a large airport, and I had no idea where to go; I hadn't been in one of these for a few years, and I was a bit disoriented for a while until I looked up and noticed the signs, then felt dumb. After several missed calls and taking forever to figure out where the baggage claim was, I made it down the correct flight of stairs and was met by an enormous assortment of people, all waiting for their luggage to arrive. It had been a smart move to pack my papers, with my small assortment of tarot decks, and tools for my personal practice, in the bag that went above my seat. Personally, it was more important than the handful of clothes I was still waiting on. Although, it was still odd to me how I'd struggled to get them to hand over my birth certificate that's until I looked at it and realized they'd forged nearly everything. Instead of my mother's name, she'd put her own, and instead of my father's, there was his.

I wasn't worried about the latter part; Dad had done a good job raising me, and it's thanks to his quick thinking that I am still alive. He'd taken time to explain and teach me things in ways he knew I would understand. He knew I would always be a bit different, so he tried to give me an upper hand.

I smiled to myself as people started to give me strange looks for blasting heavy metal through my earbuds, but it kept me calm. A couple minutes went by before spotting my friend walking aimlessly in the crowd; they were directly on the other side, and eventually I decided to call them. After joking about it for a few moments, I grabbed my remaining bag, and we headed out the door. I passed out in the car and only woke up when it was time to assess my new surroundings. Soon, we entered a home, and I didn't realize it then, but this would be the one I moved into during my stay. They had four different animals: two older cats and two seemingly newborn pups. I remember looking at them and thinking they were a bit small to already be separated from their mother, and as it would turn out, I was right; they were given up several weeks too soon, and it's not to say I don't like dogs I just prefer cats instead. Time passed, and pretty soon it was time to head to my friend's place; unfortunately, I would end up singing a different tune a couple weeks later.

Upon entering the house, I was told I'd be given the bed. This meant I was given the sole responsibility to keep the house spiritually protected, and I didn't want that. I didn't have the strength or the clear-mindedness to do so.

It was only yesterday that I left behind nearly three years of my life and put aside the pursuit of my career for the sake of mental health. Funny enough, my ex had dared me to go after my dreams, and eventually I went from being rejected by agencies and small businesses alike to modeling for the café I'd once worked at and doing frequent tarot readings for the mayor and his wife. I loved it and got to meet all sorts of people. As it turned out, I hadn't been enough, so the choice was made that I would leave, heal, and start over somewhere else.

Before long, our routine was established, and my friend ended up definitely not being a morning person; I was deeply depressed at the time, so it didn't matter. A couple weeks went by before I was informed they hadn't told anyone I was coming out. I panicked before telling them a few days later that I'd find somewhere else to stay; they were already ahead of me and said I'd been requested to puppy-sit for the house we'd visited once before. Hurriedly, I agreed, seeing as it was a way to distract myself and I would supposedly be getting paid; at least that's what they said. Everything was calm at first; they expected me to train and raise both pups, and I agreed to it as long as they understood it wasn't free labor. We sat down to discuss, and the recorder on my phone was on; they told me I'd be paid every two weeks for training, but that would turn into anything but the truth. After everything was said, one of them nearly fled to their room, leaving myself and the other seated at the table. Trying to distract myself from the creepy feeling of being watched, I decided to scroll through socials and respond to the few friends that I had. Pretty soon, being eyed like a piece of meat made me so uncomfortable, I decided to get up and leave. That's when he decided to say,

"You can either sleep in here or in my bed, but just so you know, the spare isn't all that comfortable or anything."

What an odd thing to say

Chapter 26

I nodded a quick thanks and began moving my bags into the spare room. He started protesting in that disturbingly nice way that made me wish the flight attendant hadn't taken my knife, which I'd had since my twenty-first birthday.

After a few days, I woke up with the unmistakable feeling to protect myself. As it became increasingly apparent there was no respect for personal space or boundaries, this feeling only intensified. In short, he gave me the creeps. A couple of weeks went by, and before long, I found myself trying to talk to them about training the pups and paying me. They didn't care, but it was interesting to hear the excuses. I found this behavior odd, so I started making a list. It quickly became evident that I wasn't just there for a physical reason. By now, it was my birthday again. I spent it alone, surrounded by animals, and drinking; I knew better but was depressed. Several hours passed before my phone started ringing. Without hesitation, I barely glanced at the number before picking up, and what I was told not only threw me for a loop but ticked me off:

"You'll sleep with anyone as long as you stay off the streets, huh?"

What. The. Fuck. A mix of emotions welled inside me, ranging from sheer confusion to blood-boiling rage, and I began to see red. I had no idea what was being said behind my back, but this was probably not the worst of it.

"What are you talking about? I stopped letting my ex touch me long before I found out he didn't know how to be committed. You of all people know I don't like being touched."

The answer I got made my blood boil:

"I heard you were sleeping with one of the two living in the house just so they wouldn't kick you out."

I growled so low I felt the girl on the end of the line begin to panic.

"Did you not hear me? I don't like to be touched, and I'm not my ex. I could easily end up back on the streets tomorrow and never bat an eye. I don't care who you heard that from, but if you choose to believe it, go hear it again, and never bother me."

Her voice shook as she confessed,

"Your ex is the one who told me. He's been talking to one of the guys you live with. Oh, and he's already engaged again."

I chuckled to myself, remembering an old conversation with my now ex-fiancé; I'd let him convince himself I was already seeing someone the day after I dumped him and only made things worse by telling him to believe everything he'd often accused me of doing. I was never like that, but he didn't need to know.

My blood was still boiling from her words, so I simply hung up before I said anything I'd regret. It took a few moments to calm down before I remembered the lists I'd created; this was just another notch on things that happened. I sighed and poured more from the bottle. I was tired and done with everything, but it wouldn't be until a few days later, by complete accident, that somebody would enter my life and it would start having meaning again.

Chapter 27

I'm not saying everything was all bad; there were times when I felt safe and times when I needed something close by. However, as is frequent in my life, those decent days were few and far between. Most of the time, I was told to do things that weren't my responsibility and made to feel more like an object than a person. I'd been sexualized by one of them but avoided like the plague by another, and the list kept growing as weeks went on. The only thing keeping me from prison was my spiritual practice and the one person who always made me feel seen, David.

Now, you might wonder how we met or got in contact it was via DM over Snapchat. I posted a photo from a past shoot on a day I'd been too depressed to socialize and got several messages; most were disgusting imagery from odd individuals, but a few were friendly. He was simple:

"You're cute 😊."

My immediate response: "Okay?" I didn't want to correct his grammar, but it brought a small smile to my face. After checking some other socials, I chatted with my only friend a motherfucker who still lives miles away but is one of the sweetest people. We used to chat all the time, whether on phone or text, sometimes falling asleep still talking.

A few months passed by, and I finally decided to start talking to him; during this time, he'd been persistent with messages, and I couldn't help but feel a little pull. It wasn't long before we were chatting as close as I used to spend talking to my friend, but lately, I had felt them beginning to pull away.

At some point during this time, I'd started receiving calls and texts from people I'd grown up with. Every single one of them was asking me when I'd be coming back. Apparently, my dad didn't want to socialize as much anymore, and my mom, who isn't just a devoted alcoholic, had gotten in trouble with her boss. I simply shrugged my shoulders and told them all a variety of "go to hell." Why would I care? They didn't want me anyway. According to her, she doesn't have a daughter. They have my golden child baby brother anyway. Why want the black sheep? None of them ever saw the error of their ways, and I knew that calling on the black sheep meant they wanted a scapegoat again. It's a shame; sometimes I can catch myself missing when we pretended to be a perfect family. Then again, I don't, because I never got enough to eat, and I was almost always covered in bruises or hiding self-inflicted wounds. Needless to say, minimum contact has been a lifesaver. It's a shame, but sometimes that's how life works. There are things I could say, but that's not necessary; time reveals all. At this point, life was relatively peaceful. I spent most of the time reading tarot and healing. Then I fell into a depressive state. Sometimes I'd lay awake, zoned out and completely numb; feeling detached from everything and everyone. For nearly three months, I hardly spoke to anyone and struggled to go through the motions of being okay. I watched friends start to walk away as several messages went directly from,

Omg, are you okay? Please talk to me... imu 😖

Straight into long paragraphs about what a terrible person I was or how it was obvious I didn't care. There were a few people who didn't leave and didn't go from pretending to worry to showing their true colors; among them, only one stood out, and that was the guy who had called me cute while misspelling you're.

After months of enduring the rather odd behavior and complaining to him, I was finally ready to leave everything behind. Of course, I would be taking my two kittens, but the guilt of leaving the other animals with them weighed heavily. I didn't want to leave them, but there wasn't much choice. They thought it was acceptable to chain the pups outside for days, with no proper shelter and no means to make them one. I let them sleep in the home when they weren't around, but as soon as they'd come back, both pups were out right back outside. I watched as they became lethargic, rejecting both food and water; it turned my stomach, and I pray someone else has them now, because if they'd do it to an animal, they wouldn't hesitate to do it to a person. This is one of the few rules that I live by.

I won't forget my first winter on the street when I'd accidentally stumbled on couples walking together in the snow that were holding hands. This was before anything had started, and for a second I had some hope that my first love would make good on his promise. However, just like the older brother who said he wouldn't leave, that promise quickly became null and void. He'd already moved on without a second thought, and in turn, I showed myself how to do the same. It hurts, but it also helps in a way. If things had happened the way I'd once hoped, who knows; but if you knew what would happen, would you continue life the way you have been?

Life is supposed to be unpredictable, but I've noticed most people choose to remain sheltered. Memories of the past often flood my mind, and sometimes I can find the version of myself that's trapped there. The version who will never understand why because she can't move ahead in time. Usually, she's still standing near the platform, watching people walking and holding hands; the wishful dreaming long turned into agonizing pain. Her black puff coat, wool hat, and scarves do little to keep out the cold; a smile spreads across her face, but by now it's grown sad. Silent tears stream down her face as she quietly begs to understand why nobody wants to love her. She doesn't turn away from people watching and doesn't bother wiping away the tears. They're the only thing that's warm, at least for the time being. As I look at her, forever trapped at seventeen, tears begin to fall like rain, and I try explaining that she has always been loved. If not by another person, then by me, but of course, she never believes this. We go through the motions of an argument until eventually I'm holding the younger version of myself. As she weeps uncontrollably, I feel my heart shatter, but I keep telling her that she's always been loved. The entire time she screams profanities and keeps calling me a liar. The words cut like a knife, but I keep repeating the same thing over and over again,

I love you because you are me, and it doesn't matter who decides to leave our life. I am not going anywhere.

I continue to hold her, and after several seconds, I start to feel her acceptance. She looks up and smiles; it's the first time in years that she doesn't hide our goofy grin. She lets me wipe her tears, and soon she's standing. I remind her that I love her, and this time there are no tears; instead, I feel an old wound finally begin to close.

Although I love what I do, I have to be fully present, and for that, I need to accept every part of myself. This hasn't always been easy, and I've watched many people leave, so I've given the same attentiveness to myself especially when depression hits and memories begin to resurface. Sometimes reflection leads to places where you learn what parts of you got broken, and fixing those pieces leads you to become who you're supposed to be. I left an extremely toxic family dynamic years ago and have maintained little to no contact. I'm not a stranger to leaving, and it's almost sad to say, I've grown quite good at it. I trust the process, and whatever happens, there's always a reason.

Chapter 28

I can't help but remember that day I realized I'd gotten those gifts from my mother; I can see, speak with, and hear the dead, I can speak with angels and demons, I know before things happen, and I can tell you the worst things you're trying to hide. I'm not sure when these gifts started taking the front row; I just know I made this mistake of telling someone, and this person was an old friend of my dad's one of those overly religious types and she'd often come to the house just to take me to a little church. That church was where I'd gotten assaulted for the first time, and where I would learn it was wrong to be born a girl. She took me there because I "needed it." After that day, the viewpoint shifted, and I wasn't welcome anymore; it was the pastor's foster boy who did it, but I got blamed and was later beaten. Afterwards, my hair was cut short and kept that way. My short hair would end up making it so I'd often be mistaken for a boy; this made me hate myself even more as I'd be reminded of the incident.

All through my schooling years, it was short because she made sure of it. Of course, she was the one who'd originally cut it and sometimes she'd use the incident as a means against me. I hated her but back then couldn't do anything. So, music became my escape. I started writing songs, poetry, short stories, whatever I could think up, I'd write it down. Except after my best friend passed on and my encounter with Divine, I stopped writing music for a while. The last song I wrote was found by my French teacher; it'd gotten stuck between the pages of my homework, and I told her to keep it. I wouldn't begin writing music again until I found another friend who ended up living in a different state. It was during school that I met him. He wanted to be an artist and ended up stumbling upon some lyrics he was working on at the time. He sought assistance, so I sent a quick message, and we ended up writing who knows how many songs before I lost him as well. The last thing I knew, we were seventeen, and he'd been hit during a drive-by; they got him and his daughter. I've never been sure if he's still alive or dead, and it often hurts too much to think about. So, I guess you could say there are several reasons and choices that helped shape who I am. Although I was a kid back then, that doesn't excuse the damage I caused to those who didn't deserve it. Just the same, it doesn't excuse the things that were done to me, some of which I've mentioned, and some I never will. Still, it happened, and nobody can change the past.

You'd probably think its crazy, but I never got to know anything about myself, and I wasn't interested; until everything happened that is. Only recently have I learned to embrace being a little different. While most were growing up being typical children and then teenagers, I was often playing down by the creek and in the woods behind my grandparents' house. Sometimes, I'd challenge the local wood fae to a race, from the beginning of my aunt's garden to the start of the road; fae are beings that most people cannot see, and if they can, they don't interact with them. They're the type of creature, although relatively peaceful, you don't want them to know your name or be in your house. Ironic, some of them helped raise me and often appeared as little Egyptian children. Many deities and different species have appeared this way throughout the years, at least to me. Although, they didn't like my baby brother too much. This was due to an accident while sledding one Christmas. I was eleven and my brother was nine. We grabbed our sleds and headed outside behind auntie's house. There were trees everywhere, but we didn't mind; my brother went first aiming for the biggest tree at the edge of the grass trail that led to the chicken coop and the garden. I watched as he slid down white snow, and before he got to the dip in the treeline, he planted his foot to stop himself. A bright smile flashed across my face as I grabbed my board to follow suit; it didn't go too well for me. As I slid, I knew I was going too fast, and the smile quickly vanished as I smacked headfirst into the tree. I screamed in pain, and my brother quickly got off his board and headed towards the house, screaming for help. Beautiful white snow began to turn red with the hot blood that poured from my face. I broke my nose for the first time. A few years later, as a teenager, I'd end up breaking it again by accident. Then after that, it wouldn't be me breaking my bones.

My grandma was the first out the patio door and down the steps, and she screamed when she saw me. I'd already gotten up and grabbed my snowboard; it didn't hurt, but I balled up a fist full of snow and held onto the broken part just the same. I already had an unusually high pain tolerance, but after that, most winters became a light dusting with plenty of green still sticking out. We'd hardly see that level again until I'd turned thirteen and my brother was eleven; it caused a power outage, where my dad would end up setting a standard that nobody has reached. Most of those younger years, Dad would look after my baby brother and me. Especially since she often taught overseas; since our little incident, she'd do whatever she could to avoid getting close. That meant taking on extra time, going to another country, or getting up earlier for her morning run. Whenever we were around each other, it was like two cats fighting over the last fish in the ocean. Part of me still wanted the family I'd dreamed of, but that would never happen; we only got along a handful of times, and the last time I tried to contact her shattered any hope left of establishing a relationship. It was over email and a few months before I'd decided to stop holding off my ambitions. I told her that I loved her and that I was safe; her response was that she didn't know me and she never had a daughter. I guess I wasn't as controllable as she'd originally thought. Although I've been over some of the things that happened, part of me is still grateful she was never able to take the proper place of a mother. It might sound crazy and a bit harsh, but no matter how much I say I'd wanted her to be able to, I know that's not entirely true, and it didn't matter what lies were told nobody can take my mother's place.

Oh, I heard it all growing up, and before I left for the last time. According to everyone else, the law had,

"Stepped up and did its job…"

Only, there's a few problems with that statement. She hadn't wanted to leave us but had because she thought it was the right way to go. She also had never been a drug addict, and she didn't commit suicide. She was divinely gifted, like me, only those around her had been successful at siphoning everything. They'd taken her energy, her essence, and when they couldn't get anything else, they'd gotten rid of her. They tried to do the same to me and ultimately failed. She'd also never been a midnight walker; that was another lie they'd tried to etch into our brains from an early age. I always thought it odd how they'd started when I was young by trying to convince me she was a terrible person, but every time I asked about her, there would be episodes of violence taken out on me. My baby brother and I aren't half-siblings either; he had her last name, and I got my father's. If we were, then how would you explain us having the exact same bloodline gifts? Bloodline gifts are passed down from having the same parents. Only, he doesn't want to use his, and I couldn't imagine a life without mine.

Sometimes I still think it's a bit ironic how I got my start as a witch because of the Catholic Church. On the day I thought Divine had left me, my first holy communion, my dress was small and white, with little gloves that went all the way up to my elbows; I wore tiny black shoes, with little white socks, and my white veil that covered the back of my head. My hair was long then and the incident hadn't yet happened. However, that would soon change. As we were preparing for the ceremony, the pastor's boy came in unannounced. Of course, we all panicked and started hiding ourselves, but he'd already been watching me for a while, and he was old enough to know exactly what he was about to do. He was almost old enough to move below the church where middle schoolers went for their classes.

Anyways, several of the girls had decided to escape while they could. I didn't get that memo, and it wouldn't be long before he'd end up having his way. It hurt, badly; I wanted to scream, but his hand was clamped shut over my mouth, and he didn't let up until he was done. Blood began pouring from me, but all he did was smile and whisper two words that would forever haunt me,

"Thank you."

Then he got up and walked away. It took a few minutes for someone to come looking but none too quickly for my mom to slap me across the face. She yelled and screamed, but I couldn't hear a word. Her eyes glazed over with rage, and at that moment, I felt completely abandoned. It wouldn't be until years later that I'd finally come to understand Divine had never left. Even after the attempts I'd eventually take against my own life, the attempts by those I thought I could trust, and the accidents I found myself in. Everything happens the way it was supposed to. Although I'll never remember what she said, I remember blacking out later that same day and causing her to weep for hours.

I'm also unsure if I'll ever come across the man who beat me. Then again, who would really want that? However, I am grateful for him, and I know how crazy that sounds, but he was one of the few people that didn't lie to me. He told me exactly who he was and about his past.

Although, I've noticed that whenever I've brought up how he was blatantly honest, it tends to tick people off, and it doesn't take a genius to know why. Regardless of the history.

Just the same, I always found it odd when one of my former housemates would often make the odd remark,

"I'm not the only one in this relationship…"

Though we were never in one to begin with, but asking him to stop proved useless. As did reminding his friends that I had been celibate, single, and trying to heal.

Everyone wanted to believe the liar but I'm used to that; like how my adoptive parents are saints to all those who don't truly know them. If asked, they'd deny putting hands on me or doing anything that shouldn't have been done. Except, they always had this odd habit of documenting it. For everything they did to cause me pain, they'd take a photo of it first and laugh as they wrote down how much fun it was for them.

They are part of the main reason I'll never believe my mother's or grandmother's deaths were natural or accidents. People so evil are rarely judged by man because of the pull they have, and it doesn't matter how much they've done. This realization used to be extremely upsetting before I remembered that in the end, we all get judged and answer to Divine.

That being said, if you wanted me to be nice, then you should've treated me better, and if you were looking for an apology, no anger you feel towards me can hold a candle to the regret for the things I did to those who didn't deserve it. I'm not perfect, and I've never claimed to be. I am human, and it's sad to say that I'm prone to remember the bad over the good because there were good days too. Although those were few and far between, and nearly every good moment would quickly become tainted; much like Christmas when I was sixteen.

Chapter 29

Holidays are still not my favorite, and I try not to celebrate them. That's mostly due to what would happen around those times. The verbal and sometimes physical abuse would increase, then that "special" day would come, something nice would be given to me, and I'd be reminded that I was a horrible person who didn't deserve the kindness of being alive. Interestingly enough, they never behaved like this toward my brother, but if they had, I would've made them regret it. It doesn't matter that we haven't seen or spoken to each other in years; it will always be my instinctive drive to protect him, even though I can't do that anymore.

That morning, I woke up to Lyann, my adoptive mother, coming in to turn on the lights. Her fake cheerful voice ignited over the fact that it was Christmas Day. I pulled the blankets up over my head, completely content to ignore her and go back to sleep. Unfortunately, Paul had also come downstairs. This was one of the few times I'd slept in my bed or even my room. Usually, it was on the cold concrete floor with maybe a blanket and a couch cushion for a pillow. Then again, it was one of the few times Dad was home, so things were different. This was also the same year the discussion was had about me returning to the farm alone. At first, she didn't want me to go; I agreed right away for two reasons: she wouldn't be able to touch me, and I rather liked my own company.

Dad grabbed the corner of the blanket not being held down by my tiny frame and lifted it slightly. He had a giant grin on his face, and I knew he was about to do something. Sure enough, a snowball landed on my head, and he started laughing. I smiled, sat up, and began looking for my slippers. After noticing I was getting up, they both turned to leave my room and began pestering my brother, Noah.

I mentally sighed at the missing door, remembering how I'd kicked a giant hole in it all thanks to that brat. He'd run into my room after school, knowing he had no reason to be in there, then began pulling up the blinds and messing with my things. He switched the stereo Dad had given me to some stupid country station and put my amp in front of the door. After knocking and reminding him how spoiled he was, I did the unthinkable and kicked a hole through the door with my heavy black boot. At the time, I had no idea it was hollow, but this realization would strike me quickly and only thought about how much trouble I'd gotten myself into. It wasn't bad, though; I just got reminded I was a worthless waste of space, made to walk barefoot in the snow, and then they removed my door.

My brother? Oh, he could do no wrong and was the poster child of perfection in their eyes. Maybe that's why I completely dropped contact with her at least. I still talk to Dad on rare occasions but can't help remembering the last thing he told me:

"If you ever decide to leave, you are dead to this family."

Since leaving this last time, I've basically acted as if they're already dead, so it all works out. They can pretend to be perfect, and I'll make them believe I don't know all their dirtiest secrets especially his. I never got along with Lyann, and she will never be my mother. However, I appreciate how Paul tried to be a dad.

A prime example was that day. We had a tradition every few years where one of us would have a Christmas themed around what we liked. That year was my turn, and although they never really got to know me, he at least tried. My brother met me at the bottom of the stairs, and I raced him up. Even as teenagers, sometimes we still acted like kids.

While their priority was gathering around the tree and listening to music, mine was food. I walked into the kitchen to see Dad's half-finished Christmas feast and decided to wait on the goodness by eating a bowl of chocolate cereal. After eating at the table, I joined my brother on the couch. You could tell right away that the theme was what they assumed represented me: several presents wrapped in black and white paper with a sort of Gothic look. This contrasted greatly with their bright gifts and almost made me uncomfortable. After a pause, Dad cleared his throat and ushered me to sit cross-legged on the floor. It was my turn to pass out gifts, so I started with the brat and worked around until we all had piles. Once again, I was ushered by dad to begin unwrapping what I'd gotten. So, I started with the smallest one, assuming it was a new book or something, but it wasn't. They'd gotten me passes to see one of my all-time favorite bands. I stared for several minutes at the laminate badges in my hand; they couldn't tell if I was happy, but inside I was screaming with joy. Dad put his hand on my shoulder and smiled:

"We know how much they mean to you, kiddo, and we'll go see them together. Just you and me."

I flashed him a quick grin and turned to look at the lead singer. Whenever I got overwhelmed, I'd turn on one of their songs, and his voice kept me calm; especially when everything else made no sense. Not to mention, they're incredibly talented, and I will always be a fan. The next things I received were a brand-new hoodie, a couple of tees, and their latest album. I felt like the coolest kid ever. Needless to say, I spent that day wrapped in their hoodie and listening to that album on repeat. It was one of the happiest days of my life no snide comments, hints, or malice. It was absolutely perfect.

Chapter 30

Flash forward several years, and I finally left that small town in Tennessee not before meeting a few people and stumbling upon the small church nearly directly behind the house. I never went inside, opting instead to watch the spirits that haunt the area, most of whom, ironically, weren't religiously inclined before passing. Once again, my boundaries were crossed, and I was made to feel like an object. So, I spoke to David, the one person who cared to listen, and to my surprise, I got a response something like this:

"Pack your bags. I'm coming for you. You can't be there anymore."

What was more surprising was my one-word answer:

"Okay."

After packing the few things I had, all that remained was to count the days. In less than a week, I would no longer be there. When the day came, it was filled with anxiety as he ended up turning into the neighbor's driveway and later blew a tire. Although, for the most part, it went smoothly, and when we finally met in person, it felt like we'd always known each other. Everything felt surprisingly natural, and after getting settled, I made sure both kittens were safely asleep in the backseat before giving a slight hug to one of the people I'd lived with for nearly a year. We said our goodbyes and started heading up, listening to our favorite bands and switching topics seamlessly.

Time flew by, and soon we were traveling down a back road, looking for a place to stop to get some sleep for a couple of hours. That wouldn't happen, of course, because before I knew it, he'd fallen asleep at the wheel and we started drifting off the road. Luckily, it was early morning, so no one was around. Where sleep had almost overtaken me, panic struck as I shook him awake.

"Hey, come on. You gotta wake up."

At the sound of my panicked voice and slight shaking, he jolted awake. By now, we'd drifted into the grass-filled medium. The car shook slightly as a tire blew out, and both kittens jumped up onto the backseat, surprised. They looked at me panicked, and I assured them everything would be alright. Then he began looking for a spare, and I crossed the road to do some country kid stuff. After I was done, I headed back to the car, where he told me there wasn't a spare. Great. That meant we'd have to wait for a tow truck.

Several minutes passed, and eventually, I was woken to the flashing lights of the tow truck. It was early morning; I was tired and cranky but still gathered both kittens tightly and slid into the backseat. After less than an hour and a nice nap, I was woken again by the airport lights.

Double great we'd just gone the opposite way. I watched as he got out of the tow truck until he disappeared from view; then I realized my phone was dead. Inwardly, I sighed and tried to ignore the fact my ass was hurting. After about twenty minutes, he came back and told me to gather the kittens while he took my belongings. We thanked the tow truck driver and hurried across the street to find the other car. The kittens hadn't been outside in the cold and hated every second of it. Thankfully, it wouldn't be for long, as we rounded the corner and I put them in the backseat of another By now, all of us remained awake, and soon we were approaching the lights of another town. Neither of us noticed that at some point during the drive, we'd raised the music a little louder; we were getting looks. Nothing seemed to matter, even as I felt everything shift. At some point, I'd fallen asleep during the drive and only stirred when we pulled up to the apartments. I didn't bother to get an initial feel for the place; all I wanted was to go back to sleep. After bringing the kittens in, I did just that.

A couple of weeks passed, and a much better routine was established: waking early every morning, drinking coffee, doing tarot, talking with people in my industry, and planning the next steps ahead. I've even met David's family and celebrated both Yule and New Year's in a much more positive light.

I leave the past in the past all that which shaped who I am. That mindset and behavior protected me for a time, but now I've let go of only living strictly for survival.

This is the most difficult part but it'll be worth it.

I did what I had to do to stay alive. Most of what I went through, and a few people I knew briefly, I've decided to hardly mention, if sometimes and hopefully at all and that's just the way it stays.

I've made mistakes and been taught immediate lessons.

Although sometimes I wish I could be a kid again and walk through the doors of my childhood home for the first time, where everything would magically be better. Some part of me will always want to say, "I'm going home to see my family," before remembering all that happened.

For every decent moment, there were far more that outweighed them. It got so bad.

I know I've said this before, but I hold the man who put his hands on me in higher regard than most people simply because of his honesty.

It doesn't matter how much twitching I do from brain misfiring or how bad the flashbacks get; it won't stop me from going after what I want.

I just wish I had a family to go back to sometimes and hopefully someday, I'll make that a reality. For now, it's time to focus. Dreams can only come true once you let go of the past and embrace the uncertainty of the fleeting moments we're given.

Although, I'll never forget the day my life was almost taken that was the turning point. That fight, argument, those words, and the decision to put down what I'd struggled with for years it almost ended everything.

I was eighteen or nineteen when I met Tyler, and twenty-one when he almost took my life. I'll forever remember that day. As it was his birthday.

We were addicts, suffering, with nothing to our names and we had nothing going for us, but I still, in the heat of anger, uttered the words that changed everything forever:

"I don't want to do this anymore."

As I held up a small bag and showed him. He had a look of confusion mixed with frustration that I'll never forget as his deep brown eyes met mine and he asked,

"What?"

Still holding the bag, I repeated,

"I don't want to do this anymore. I want to get sober."

That's exactly what I did, and I have no regrets.

To Tyler, the man who taught me painfully valuable lessons:

I'm not mad anymore. I used to be so angry at the thought of you that sometimes I'd dream of doing worse than I could've imagined. That's not who I am, though. I understand what happened between us, and I'm sorry for the part I played. The nightmares get bad sometimes but not like they were before. I remember that night in detail, and I'm not angry anymore.

Sometimes it hurts when you cross my mind, and sometimes I wonder if you're doing all right. I hope you got out of the situation we were in together, and I'm grateful for the past. It took a while, but I finally figured out what you were trying to do.

Although it was a bit of a shocking delivery. There are times when I find myself crying because I know you handled things the only way you understood, and I don't blame you.

I forgive you. Thank you for trying to help me, even if it wasn't the best way or place to do so.

To those who broke me when I needed support:

Thank you. I needed that. I wouldn't see things the way I do now if it hadn't worked out the way it did.

To Paul and Lyann, my adoptive parents:

I forgive you. You each taught me a lot of valuable things. Thank you to Lyann, who taught me how to keep people at arm's length and never put another ahead of myself, and thank you to Paul, who did his best to raise me the right way. Without your lessons and the advice I often wanted to ignore, I'm not sure where I would have ended up or if I'd still be alive. To the men who tried to sell me:

That was the quickest lesson I was ever taught. Even so, I'm forever grateful.

To anyone that I hurt as an idiot kid:

It won't mean much now, but I am sorry. I was old enough to know better but not mature enough to understand or care. I hold myself accountable now, and I hope you all have been able to figure out everything. Although it's not like it matters much; we all did stupid and hurtful things to one another.

The only difference is I didn't lie when I said I wouldn't come back, and I didn't lie when I said I was choosing to heal.

Maybe I'll come through someday, and then again, maybe I won't. Last but not least: to myself:

I'm sorry for the things I put you through and for not being able to help you when you needed it. I love you, and we got this. Whatever the future holds, we've always been the fighter and the wild child. Let's keep it that way.

I'd rather be the crazy girl that keeps going than anyone else. I'm not perfect. I'm flawed and human, and that's the way it's going to stay.

Now, after everything I've said and all I've chosen to leave out, I simply leave you with this, my favorite quote from one of the greatest minds ever known to mankind, and a thank you for coming along with me this far.

"You can't solve a problem at the same level that it was created. You have to rise above it to the next level." – Albert Einstein.

www.ingramcontent.com/pod-product-compliance
Lightning Source LLC
Chambersburg PA
CBHW061801070526
44586CB00023B/2661